The Poetry Collection

Carl Sandburg

~The Poetry Collection~

Carl Sandburg

Illustrated by
Robert Crawford

Edited by Kathryn Benzel, PhD

MoonDance

This book is dedicated to my first granddaughter, Cecilia Rose Mettey. She came into our lives at just the right time! —R. C.
For my lovely grandchildren, readers all of them: Lucia, Josiah, Caleb, Noah —K. B.

Brimming with creative inspiration, how-to projects, and useful information to enrich your everyday life, Quarto Knows is a favorite destination for those pursuing their interests and passions. Visit our site and dig deeper with our books into your area of interest: Quarto Creates, Quarto Cooks, Quarto Homes, Quarto Lives, Quarto Drives, Quarto Explores, Quarto Gifts, or Quarto Kids.

© 2018 Quarto Publishing Group USA Inc.
Original text © 2017 Kathryn Benzel
Illustrations © 2017 Robert Crawford

First Published in 2017 by Published by MoonDance Press, an imprint of The Quarto Group.
26391 Crown Valley Parkway, Suite 220, Mission Viejo, CA 92691, USA.
T (949) 380-7510 F (949) 380-7575 www.QuartoKnows.com

Walter Foster Publishing titles are also available at discount for retail, wholesale, promotional, and bulk purchase. For details, contact the Special Sales Manager by email at specialsales@quarto.com or by mail at The Quarto Group, Attn: Special Sales Manager, 100 Cummings Center, Suite 265D, Beverly, MA 01915, USA.

ISBN: 978-1-63322-151-2

Digital edition published in 2017
eISBN: 978-1-63322-425-4

Cover design and layout by Melissa Gerber

Printed in Guangdong, China
10 9 8 7 6 5 4 3 2 1
November 2019
19090228

Contents

Introduction

IT WAS A RAINY GRAY AFTERNOON IN DOWNTOWN CHICAGO, 1914. Carl Sandburg was huddled in a doorway waiting for the streetcar. He saw workers coming up from underground, in worn-out overalls, carrying their muddy shovels and lunch pails; the street vendors closing up their vegetable stands, counting their few pennies; garment workers walking slowly, their shoulders stooped, and heads hanging from twelve-hour work days; rich folk wearing their top hats in horse-drawn buggies, and new Ford automobiles buzzing around them. People's hats were blowing every which way in the slanted rain. Standing in the dreary weather, he remembered the warmth of his family and the prairie sunsets brilliant with red, orange, and yellow; harvesting farmers in the dust and sweat; and he reminisced about the whistling wind as he hung onto a boxcar as a hobo crossing the prairie. This is Carl Sandburg's poetry, filled with common Americans, the salt of the earth, working hard, living sparsely, laughing and singing a lot. He was the "Poet of the People," a spokesperson for "the mob, the crowd, the mass." He was the voice of early-20th-century American life.

Carl Sandburg was born on a cornstalk mattress in 1878 in Galesburg, Illinois, the land of Abraham Lincoln. It was America's Heartland, near Chicago's railroad intersection for American life. His parents were Swedish immigrants who never learned to read or write in English, struggling to support their seven children. Sandburg stopped his education after eighth grade to help with the family's income. He shined shoes, delivered milk and newspapers, and swept out bars and barbershops. In Chicago, he was introduced to the life and living that inspired his *Chicago Poems* (1916). At age nineteen in 1897, he hopped onto a boxcar heading west. On this trip, he discovered the breadth and beauty of the American landscape that would inspire his collections, *Cornhuskers* (1918) and *Smoke and Steel* (1920).

During his lifetime, Sandburg experienced the aftermath of the Civil War and saw the ravages of the 1960s Vietnam War. He saw the new Ford Model T in 1908 and the Ford Edsel in 1958. He lived through two depressions, including the Great Depression and the Dust Bowl. He endured two world wars. He witnessed the advent of television and was invited to fly on the first transcontinental flight from the East Coast to the West. He was a newspaper reporter, a lecturer, a biographer, and a folk singer. He won three Pulitzer Prizes for history and poetry.

Sandburg's experiences and observations are at the essence of his poetic vision, of the voice of the people. The underlying hope at the core of his poetry brings "tears for the tragic, love for the beautiful, laughter at folly, and silent, reverent contemplation of the common and everyday mysteries." He said, "Poetry is a mystic, sensuous mathematics of fire, smoke-stack, waffles, pansies, people, and purple sunsets. The capture of a picture, a song, a flair, in a deliberate prism of words."

He died in 1967 at 89, listening to Chopin and smelling the magnolias. His last word was "Paula," his wife's name.

Poems about People

Young Bullfrogs

Jimmy Wimbledon listened a first week in June.
Ditches along prairie roads of Northern Illinois
Filled the arch of night with young bullfrog songs.
Infinite mathematical metronomic croaks rose and spoke,
Rose and sang, rose in a choir of puzzles.
They made his head ache with riddles of music.
They rested his head with beaten cadence.
Jimmy Wimbledon listened.

Infinite — can't be measured because it never ends
metronomic — sounds like a device used to mark
musical time
cadence — rhythm in musical song or spoken speech

Weeds

From the time of the early radishes
To the time of the standing corn
Sleepy Henry Hackerman hoes.

There are laws in the village against weeds.
The law says a weed is wrong and shall be killed.
The weeds say life is a white and lovely thing
And the weeds come on and on in irrepressible regiments.
Sleepy Henry Hackerman hoes; and the village law uttering a ban
on weeds is unchangeable law.

irrepressible — wild, disorderly
regiments — strong troops

Soup

I saw a famous man eating soup.
I say he was lifting a fat broth

Into his mouth with a spoon.
His name was in the newspapers that day

Spelled out in tall black headlines
And thousands of people were talking about him.

When I saw him,
He sat bending his head over a plate
Putting soup in his mouth with a spoon.

I Am the People, the Mob

I am the people — the mob — the crowd — the mass.

Do you know that all the great work of the world is done through me?

I am the workingman, the inventor, the maker of the world's food and clothes.

I am the audience that witnesses history. The Napoleons come from me and the Lincolns. They die. And then I send forth more Napoleons and Lincolns.

I am the seed ground. I am a prairie that will stand for much plowing. Terrible storms pass over me. I forget. The best of me is sucked out and wasted. I forget. Everything but Death comes to me and makes me work and give up what I have. And I forget.

Sometimes I growl, shake myself and spatter a few red drops for history to remember. Then — I forget.

When I, the People, learn to remember, when I, the People, use the lessons of yesterday and no longer forget who robbed me last year, who played me for a fool — then there will be no speaker in all the world say the name: "The People," with any fleck of a sneer in his voice or any far-off smile of derision.

The mob — the crowd — the mass — will arrive then.

Napoleons — Napoleon Bonaparte (1769-1821), French political leader, emperor of France from 1804-1814
seed ground — cultivated land where crops are planted
sneer — expression of contempt

Shenandoah

In the Shenandoah Valley, one rider gray and one rider blue, and the sun
on the riders wondering.

Piled in the Shenandoah, riders blue and riders gray, piled with shovels,
one and another, dust in the Shenandoah taking them quicker than
mothers take children done with play.

The blue nobody remembers, the gray nobody remembers, it's all old and
old nowadays in the Shenandoah.

. . .

And all is young, a butter of dandelions slung on the turf, climbing blue
flowers of the wishing woodlands wondering: a midnight purple violet
claims the sun among old heads, among old dreams of repeating heads of a
rider blue and a rider gray in the Shenandoah.

Shenandoah Valley — West Virginia, site of Civil War battles (1861-1865)
rider gray — Confederate or Southern soldiers during Civil War
rider blue— Union or Northern soldiers during Civil War
slung — thrown about

Paula

Nothing else in this song — only your face.
Nothing else here — only your drinking, night-gray eyes.

The pier runs into the lake straight as a rifle barrel.
I stand on the pier and sing how I know you mornings.
It is not your eyes, your face, I remember.
It is not your dancing, race-horse feet.
It is something else I remember you for on the pier mornings.

Your hands are sweeter than nut-brown bread when you touch me.
Your shoulder brushes my arm — a south-west wind crosses the pier.
I forget your hands and your shoulder and I say again:

Nothing else in this song — only your face.
Nothing else here — only your drinking, night-gray eyes.

Paula — Carl's wife; they married in 1908.

Manual System

Mary has a thingamajig clamped on her ears
And sits all day taking plugs out and sticking plugs in.
Flashes and flashes — voices and voices
                    calling for ears to put words in
Faces at the ends of wires asking for other faces
                    at the ends of other wires:
All day taking plugs out and sticking plugs in,
Mary has a thingamajig clamped on her ears.

Manual System — Early telephone communication (1876-1904) used switchboard operators to connect callers. The caller would be connected to a central location, and the operator would plug that call into the person being called.
thingamajig — something hard to name

Jazz Fantasia

Drum on your drums, batter on your banjoes,
sob on the long cool winding saxophones.
Go to it, O jazzmen.

Sling your knuckles on the bottoms of the happy
tin pans, let your trombones ooze, and go husha-
husha-hush with the slippery sand-paper.

Moan like an autumn wind high in the lonesome treetops,
moan soft like you wanted somebody terrible, cry like a
racing car slipping away from a motorcycle cop, bang-bang!
you jazzmen, bang altogether drums, traps, banjoes, horns,
tin cans — make two people fight on the top of a stairway
and scratch each other's eyes in a clinch tumbling down the stairs.

Can the rough stuff . . . now a Mississippi steamboat pushes
up the night river with a hoo-hoo-hoo-oo . . . and the green
lanterns calling to the high soft stars . . . a red moon rides
on the humps of the low river hills . . . go to it, O jazzmen.

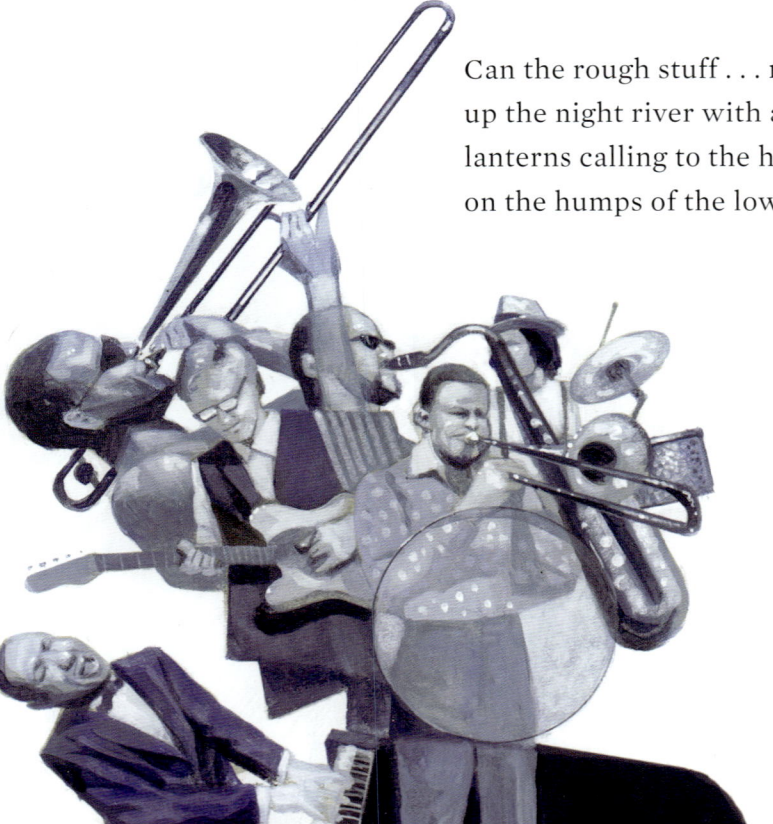

*Jazz — a type of music that originated in New
Orleans, Louisiana, in the early 20th century
Fantasia — free-form musical composition;
something that is fanciful
Can — stop, dismiss*

Illinois Farmer

Bury this old Illinois farmer with respect.
He slept the Illinois nights of his life after days of work in Illinois cornfields.
Now he goes on a long sleep.
The wind he listened to in the cornsilk and tassels, the wind that
combed his red beard zero mornings when snow lay white on the
yellow ears in the bushel basket at the corncrib,
The same wind will now blow over the place here where his hands must
dream of Illinois corn.

cornsilk — fine tassels on the top of ears of corn

Buffalo Bill

Boy heart of Johnny Jones — aching today?
Aching, and Buffalo Bill in town?
Buffalo Bill and ponies, cowboys, Indians?

Some of us know
All about it, Johnny Jones.

Buffalo Bill is a slanting look of the eyes,
   A slanting look under a hat on a horse.
He sits on a horse and a passing look is fixed
   On Johnny Jones, you and me, barelegged,
A slanting, passing, careless look under a hat on a horse.

Go clickety-clack, O pony hoofs along the street.
Come on and slant your eyes again, O Buffalo Bill.
Give us again the ache of our boy hearts.
Fill us again with the red love of prairies, dark nights, lonely wagons, and
   the crack-crack of rifles sputtering flashes into an ambush.

Buffalo Bill (1846-1917) — an early pony express rider, served in the Union army during the Civil War, created Buffalo Bill's Wild West show
slanting — at an angle

Early Moon

The baby moon, a canoe, a silver papoose canoe, sails and sails in the
   Indian west.
A ring of silver foxes, a mist of silver foxes, sit and sit around the Indian
   moon.
One yellow star for a runner, and rows of blue stars for more runners,
   keep a line of watchers.
O foxes, baby moon, runners, you are the panel of memory, fire-white
   writing tonight of the Red Man's dreams.
Who squats, legs crossed and arms folded, matching its look against
   the moon-face, the star-faces, of the West?
Who are the Mississippi Valley ghosts, of copper foreheads, riding wiry
   ponies in the night? — no bridles, love-arms on the pony necks, rid-
   ding in the night a long old trail?
Why do they always come back when the silver foxes sit around the
   early moon, a silver papoose, in the Indian west?

papoose — an infant or very young child in Native American culture
Indian moon — In Native American thought, each month was described as a type of
moon (e.g., Moose Hunter Moon, Corn Maker Moon, Freezing River Maker Moon).

Branches

The dancing girls here . . . after a long night of it . . .
The long beautiful night of the wind and rain in April,
The long night hanging down from the drooping branches of the top of
    a birch tree,
Swinging, swaying, to the wind for a partner, to the rain for a partner.
What is the humming, swishing thing they sing in the morning now?
The rain, the wind, the swishing whispers of the long slim curve so little
    and so dark on the western morning sky . . . these dancing girls
    here on an April early morning . . .
They have had a long cool beautiful night of it with their partners learning
    this year's song of April.

Washerwoman

The washerwoman is a member of the Salvation Army.
And over the tub of suds rubbing underwear clean
She sings that Jesus will wash her sins away
And the red wrongs she has done God and man
Shall be white as driven snow.
Rubbing underwear she sings of the Last Great Washday.

Salvation Army — an international charitable organization founded by Methodists in 1865 in London. They seek donations, especially at Christmastime, when volunteers ring their bells by red buckets.
Last Great Washday — a metaphor for Final Judgment Day

Psalm of Those Who Go Forth before Daylight

The policeman buys shoes slow and careful; the teamster buys gloves slow and careful; they take care of their feet and hands; they live on their feet and hands.

The milkman never argues; he works alone and no one speaks to him; the city is asleep when he is on his job; he puts a bottle on six hundred porches and calls it a day's work; he climbs two hundred wooden stairways; two horses are company for him; he never argues.

The rolling-mill men and the sheet-steel men are brothers of cinders; they empty cinders out of their shoes after the day's work; they ask their wives to fix burnt holes in the knees of their trousers; their necks and ears are covered with a smut; they scour their necks and ears; they are brothers of cinders.

Psalm — sacred song or poem of praise
rolling-mill men and sheet-steel men — they make metal
into flat pieces used in construction of cars and airplanes,
tin roofs. Smaller, thinner metal like gold and silver is used
to make jewelry.

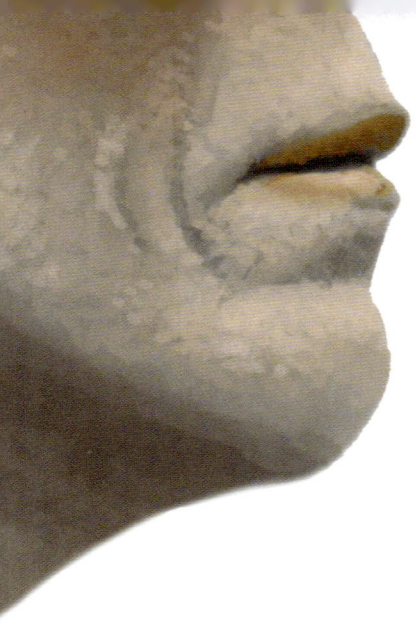

People with Proud Chins

I tell them where the wind comes from,
Where the music goes when the fiddle is in the box.

Kids — I saw one with a proud chin, a sleepyhead,
And the moonline creeping white on her pillow.
 I have seen their heads in the starlight
 And their proud chins marching in a mist of stars.

They are the only people I never lie to.
 I give them honest answers,
Answers shrewd as the circles of white on brown chestnuts.

shrewd — good at judging people and events; clever

Hits and Runs

I remember the Chillicothe ball players grappling the Rock Island ball
    players in a sixteen-inning game ended by darkness.
And the shoulders of the Chillicothe players were a red smoke against the
    sundown and the shoulders of the Rock Island players were a yellow
    smoke against the sundown.
And the umpire's voice was hoarse calling balls and strikes and outs and
    the umpire's throat fought in the dust for a song.

*Chillicothe and Rock Island — towns in Illinois where minor league baseball teams played
sixteen-inning games — usually ball games consist of nine innings; this game has been tied since the
ninth inning and the teams continue to play for a winner.*

Poems about Places

Fog

The fog comes
on little cat feet.

It sits looking
over harbor and city
on silent haunches
and then moves on.

haunches — the upper part of an animal's rear legs

Young Sea

The sea is never still.
It pounds on the shore
Restless as a young heart,
Hunting.

The sea speaks
And only the stormy hearts
Know what it says:
It is the face
      of a rough mother speaking.

*hoar — a weather phenomenon
in which ice crystals or water
vapor freezes over objects and
vegetation*

The sea is young.
One storm cleans all the hoar
And loosens the age of it.
I hear it laughing, reckless.

They love the sea,
Men who ride on it
And know they will die
Under the salt of it.

Let only the young come,
      Says the sea.
Let them kiss my face
      And hear me.
I am the last word
      And I tell
Where storms and stars come from.

Who Am I?

My head knocks against the stars.
My feet are on the hilltops.
My finger-tips are in the valleys and shores of universal life.
Down in the sounding foam of primal things I reach my hands and play
    with pebbles of destiny.
I have been to hell and back many times.
I know all about heaven, for I have talked with God.
I dabble in the blood and guts of the terrible.
I know the passionate seizure of beauty
And the marvelous rebellion of man at all signs reading "Keep Off."

My name is Truth and I am the most elusive captive in the universe.

universal life — life everywhere in the world
sounding foam — the sound of waves on the beach
primal things — things at the beginning of life or the world
destiny — the future; fate
passionate seizure — strong emotional grasp
elusive captive — hard-to-find prisoner or hostage

The Road and the End

I shall foot it
Down the roadway in the dusk,
Where shapes of hunger wander
And the fugitives of pain go by.
I shall foot it
In the silence of the morning,
See the night slur into dawn,
Hear the slow great winds arise
Where tall trees flank the way
And shoulder toward the sky.

The broken boulders by the road
Shall not commemorate my ruin.
Regret shall be the gravel under foot.
I shall watch for
Slim birds swift of wing
That go where wind and ranks of thunder
Drive the wild processionals of rain.

The dust of the traveled road
Shall touch my hands and face.

fugitives — people who run away
slur — smear + blur = slur
flank — stand next to something
shoulder — nudge
commemorate — honor
regret — something you feel sorry for
ranks of thunder — like soldiers standing in formation
processionals — formal celebrations or parades

Sunset from Omaha Hotel Window

Into the blue river hills
The red sun runners go
And the long sand changes
And today is a goner
And today is not worth haggling over.

    Here in Omaha
    The gloaming is bitter
    As in Chicago
    Or Kenosha.

The long sand changes.
To-day is a goner.
Time knocks in another brass nail.
Another yellow plunger shoots the dark.

    Constellations
    Wheeling over Omaha
    As in Chicago
    Or Kenosha.

The long sand is gone
and all the talk is stars.
They circle in a dome over Nebraska.

runners — streamers
long sand — reference to the prehistoric
time when the prairies were under water
haggling — arguing
Omaha — city in Nebraska
Kenosha — city in Wisconsin
gloaming — twilight, dusk
goner — dead
brass nail — used in coffins because they don't rust
plunger — pointer or indicator
Constellations — groups of stars forming shapes,
like the Big Dipper
wheeling — turning, revolving

Limited

I am riding on a limited express, one of the crack trains of the nation.
Hurtling across the prairie into blue haze and dark air go fifteen all-steel
    coaches holding a thousand people.
(All the coaches shall be scrap and rust and all the men and women
    laughing in the diners and sleepers shall pass to ashes.)
I ask a man in the smoker where he is going and he answers: "Omaha."

limited express — a fast train with few stops
crack trains — excellent trains
hurtling — going fast, racing
haze — mist or fog
diners and sleepers — special cars on a train
for eating and sleeping

Laughing Corn

There was a high majestic fooling
Day before yesterday in the yellow corn.

And day after tomorrow in the yellow corn
There will be high majestic fooling.

The ears ripen in late summer
And come on with a conquering laughter,
Come on with a high and conquering laughter.

The long-tailed blackbirds are hoarse.
One of the smaller blackbirds chitters on a stalk
And a spot of red is on its shoulder
And I never heard its name in my life.

Some of the ears are bursting.
A white juice works inside.
Cornsilk creeps in the end and dangles in the wind.
Always — I never knew it any other way —
The wind and the corn talk things over together.
And the rain and the corn and the sun and the corn
Talk things over together.

Over the road is the farmhouse.
The siding is white and a green blind is slung loose.
It will not be fixed till the corn is husked.
The farmer and his wife talk things over together.

fooling — tricking, joking, playful
hoarse — having a rough, grating sound
chitters — chatters, chirps
cornsilk — fine tassels on the top of ears of corn
slung — open, broken
husked — removed the husk (outer green leaves of corn)

Muckers

Twenty men stand watching the muckers.
> Stabbing the sides of the ditch
> Where clay gleams yellow,
> Driving the blades of their shovels
> Deeper and deeper for the new gas mains,
> Wiping sweat off their faces
> > With red bandanas.

The muckers work on . . . pausing . . . to pull
Their boots out of suckholes where they slosh.

> Of the twenty looking on
Ten murmur, "O, it's a hell of a job,"
Ten others, "Jesus, I wish I had the job."

muckers — workers who remove dirt and waste
gleams — shines brilliantly
new gas mains — 1900-1914 in Chicago, underground
pipe systems were built to provide energy
suckholes — When muckers worked in mud, their boots
made a sucking sound when they walked.

34

Picnic Boat

Sunday night and the park policemen tell each other it is dark as a
     stack of black cats on Lake Michigan.

A big picnic boat comes home to Chicago from the peach farms of
     Saugatuck.

Hundreds of electric bulbs break the night's darkness, a flock of red and
     yellow birds with wings at a standstill.

Running along the deck-railings are festoons and leaping in curves are
     loops of light from prow and stern to the tall smokestacks.

Over the hoarse crunch of waves at my pier comes a hoarse answer in
     the rhythmic oompa of the brasses playing a Polish folk-song for the
     home-comers.

*Lake Michigan — one of the Great Lakes;
Chicago is on the southwestern shore
Saugatuck — a city in Michigan on the east
shore of Lake Michigan; in the early 20th
century, it was the destination of weekend
vacationers from all the Midwest.
festoons — garland decorations
prow — front of boat
stern — back of boat
rhythmic — having a recurring pattern of
sound*

Harvest Sunset

Red gold of pools,
Sunset furrows six o'clock,
And the farmer done in the fields
And the cows in the barns with bulging udders.

Take the cows and the farmer,
Take the barns and the bulging udders.
Leave the red gold of pools
And sunset furrows six o'clock.
The farmer's wife is singing.
The farmer's boy is whistling.
I wash my hands in red gold of pools.

furrows — trenches in plowed fields

36

Haunts

There are places I go when I am strong.
One is a marsh pool where I used to go
                       with a long-ear hound dog.
One is a wild crabapple tree; I was there
                    a moonlight night with a girl.
The dog is gone; the girl is gone; I go to these
                   places when there is no other place to go.

Theme in Yellow

I spot the hills
With yellow balls in autumn.
I light the prairie cornfields
Orange and tawny gold clusters
And I am called pumpkins.
On the last of October
When dusk is fallen

Children join hands
And circle round me
Singing ghost songs
And love to the harvest moon;
I am a jack-o'-lantern
With terrible teeth
And the children know
I am fooling.

Buffalo Dusk

The buffaloes are gone.
And those who saw the buffaloes are gone.
Those who saw the buffaloes by thousands and how they pawed the
    prairie sod into dust with their hoofs, their great heads down pawing
    on in a great pageant of dusk,
Those who saw the buffaloes are gone.
And the buffaloes are gone.

from "Smoke and Steel"

Smoke of the fields in spring is one,
Smoke of the leaves in autumn another.
Smoke of a steel-mill roof or a battleship funnel,
They all go up in a line with a smokestack,
Or they twist . . . in the slow twist . . . of the wind.

If the north wind comes they run to the south.
If the west wind comes they run to the east.
    By this sign
    all smokes
    know each other.
Smoke of the fields in spring and leaves in autumn,
Smoke of the finished steel, chilled and blue,
By the oath of work they swear: "I know you."

funnel — smokestack on a ship

Hunted and hissed from the center
Deep down long ago when God made us over,
Deep down are the cinders we came from —
You and I and our heads of smoke.

The Skyscraper Loves Night

One by one lights of a skyscraper fling their checkering cross work on the
    velvet gown of night.

I believe the skyscraper loves night as a woman and brings her playthings
    she asks for, brings her a velvet gown,
And loves the white of her shoulders hidden under the dark feel of it all.

The masonry of steel looks to the night for somebody it loves,
He is a little dizzy and almost dances . . . waiting . . . dark . . .

masonry — stonework

Valley Song

The sunset swept
To the valley's west, you remember.

The frost was on.
A star burnt blue.
We were warm, you remember,
And counted the rings on a moon.

The sunset swept
To the valley's west
And was gone in a big dark door of stars.

Between Two Hills

Between two hills
The old town stands.
The houses loom
And the roofs and trees
And the dusk and the dark,
The damp and the dew
  Are there.

The prayers are said
And the people rest
For sleep is there
And the touch of dreams
  Is over all.

The Year

I

A storm of white petals,
Buds throwing open baby fists
Into hands of broad flowers.

II

Red roses running upward,
Clambering to the clutches of life
Soaked in crimson.

III

Rabbles of tattered leaves
Holding golden flimsy hopes
Against the tramplings
into the pits and gullies.

IV

Hoarfrost and silence:
Only the muffling
Of winds dark and lonesome —
Great lullabies to the long sleepers.

rabbles — crowds, mobs
tramplings — crushing, flattening
hoarfrost — frost

River Roads

Let the crows go by hawking their caw and caw.
They have been swimming in midnights of coal mines somewhere.
Let 'em hawk their caw and caw.

Let the woodpecker drum and drum on a hickory stump.
He has been swimming in red and blue pools somewhere hundreds of
     years
And the blue has gone to his wings and the red has gone to his head.
Let his red head drum and drum.

Let the dark pools hold the birds in a looking-glass.
And if the pool wishes, let it shiver to the blur of many wings, old
     swimmers from old places.

Let the redwing streak a line of vermilion on the green wood lines.
And the mist along the river fix its purple in lines of a woman's shawl
     on lazy shoulders.

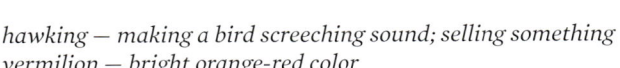

hawking — making a bird screeching sound; selling something
vermilion — bright orange-red color

Street Window

The pawn-shop man knows hunger,
And how far hunger has eaten the heart
Of one who comes with an old keepsake.
Here are wedding rings and baby bracelets,
Scarf pins and shoe buckles, jeweled garters,
Old-fashioned knives with inlaid handles,
Watches of old gold and silver,
Old coins worn with finger-marks.
They tell stories.

*pawn-shop — a shop where the pawnbroker lends
money and keeps personal property as guarantee
keepsake — souvenir; remembrance*

What Carl Was Thinking

Young Bullfrogs: Carl shows that a boy hears a bullfrog's sounds as music instead of just a croak. He demonstrates that Jimmy has an ear for music, and that it lingers in his head at the beginning of summer.

Weeds: Henry hoes his weeds because that is what the farmers in the area say must be done. Even though Henry knows the village's expectations, he still sees the strength in the weeds. And Henry knows that no amount of hoeing will ever really get rid of the weeds.

Soup: Depicting an ordinary event — eating soup — Carl shows us that all people are the same, even famous people.

I Am the People, the Mob: One of Carl's most famous poems. He rejoices in the strength and endurance of American people as they work together to maintain the American democracy.

Shenandoah: First, the Civil War battlefields from 1864 in the Shenandoah Valley are described as cemeteries where soldiers are buried. But then, after the passage of time, the fields are covered with wildflowers and grass, and speak of life.

Paula: This is Carl's love poem to his wife, Paula. He compares his poem to a song that celebrates his wife and especially her face. The song is sung from a pier to the depths of the sea.

Manual System: Imagine early telephone communication without cell phones or email. That early communication seemed like a kind of magic where people's voices materialized in odd contraptions.

Jazz Fantasia: The jazz music on a pleasure boat cruise on the Mississippi River is free-flowing and playful. Carl uses onomatopoeia as a poetic technique to create words that sound like an actual sound — "husha-husha-hush."

Illinois Farmer: The farmer wants to be buried on his own land, where he worked with his dreams.

Buffalo Bill: Buffalo Bill symbolizes the great American hero of the West. When he comes to town with his show, the parade is exciting for the young boys.

Early Moon: A baby moon, an early moon, is the beginning of the moon cycle. It looks like a small sliver or fingernail, "a canoe." This poem explores the potential of youth in terms of Native American culture.

Branches: The joy of spring is described by seeing and hearing branches move in the wind, like dancers.

Washerwoman: This washerwoman's work is like a gospel song calling for forgiveness.

Psalm of Those Who Go Forth before Daylight: We should praise those mill workers who keep our lives running smoothly through their sacrifices of backbreaking work, and little time for family and friends. They take pride in their work and never complain.

People with Proud Chins: Carl speaks about children's natural capacity to see the truth. Those children have strong chins and are not to be fooled with because they can see through lies and deceit.

Hits and Runs: Carl shows us how difficult it is for teams to play through an unusually long game, and for the umpires and fans too. When Carl was growing up in Galesburg, Illinois, he played baseball with his friends in a vacant lot.

Fog: Carl gives us a picture of fog as it creeps, stops, and moves on. It's a metaphor, comparing the fog to a slinking cat.

Young Sea: Carl imagines being young is like the movement of the sea, the salty ocean. Like the sea, a young person is restless, reckless, laughing.

Who Am I?: Carl looks for Truth in the heavens, on top of mountains, at the seashore. The natural world is a place to seek truth, knowledge of the universe.

The Road and the End: Life is like walking down a dusty path, during day or night. It is an adventure, a journey to experience the nature around us, and we get dirty with dust, with the touch of life.

Sunset from Omaha Hotel Window: Omaha, Nebraska, depicts a wide-open view of the Earth, the vast landscape of the Great Plains. Carl celebrates the wonder of this world, its past and present found where the sky meets Earth at the horizon.

Limited: In the early 20th century, limited trains were the fastest way to get from one place to another, generally stopping at larger cities, like from Chicago and Omaha. In the parentheses, Carl laments the loss of a culture when the trains are no longer useful.

Laughing Corn: "Majestic fooling" is a peculiar image that puts together unlikely ideas; a dignified joke. This poem compares the cornfield laughing playfully with the farmer and his wife.

Muckers: The muckers' work is portrayed as messy and dirty. But still people want those jobs in times of unemployment (1910s).

Picnic Boat: Carl describes the weekend pleasure boat that many Chicagoans took from Chicago across Lake Michigan to Saugatuck and Michigan's famous "Big Pavilion."

Harvest Sunset: "Red gold of pools" is mentioned three times to suggest a lovely, productive harvest.

Haunts: Carl describes the ways that places create our memories.

Theme in Yellow: Carl pretends to be a Halloween pumpkin to tell us how it might feel to be part of the Halloween celebration.

Buffalo Dusk: Carl laments the extinction of American buffaloes during the 1800s; it was a sad occasion in American history.

from "Smoke and Steel": All kinds of smoke mix together as the wind blows them. Our thoughts are like smoke that move around and mix together.

The Skyscraper Loves Night: The daytime image of the skyscraper's stone and steel falls in love with the nighttime image of the building as a graceful woman's figure wearing a sparkling evening gown.

Valley Song: As the sun sets in a valley, there is no horizon for the red, orange sunsets. We see just the slices of night in the stars above us.

Between Two Hills: People are protected by the hills that surround them and peacefully go to bed at night in a quiet village in a valley.

The Year: Each of the seasons is described from flowers and trees found at that time of year, how we see and hear those moments.

River Roads: On this road we find all kinds of birds that are full of color and sound. The birds are personified as people swimming in the nearby pool.

Street Window: All the items in a pawnshop have personal stories.

Index

THE POETRY COLLECTION

Walt Whitman

~The Poetry Collection~
Walt Whitman

Edited by
Karen Karbiener, PhD

Illustrated by Kate Evans

MoonDance

Brimming with creative inspiration, how-to projects, and useful information to enrich your everyday life, Quarto Knows is a favorite destination for those pursuing their interests and passions. Visit our site and dig deeper with our books into your area of interest: Quarto Creates, Quarto Cooks, Quarto Homes, Quarto Lives, Quarto Drives, Quarto Explores, Quarto Gifts, or Quarto Kids.

First Published in 2017 by Published by MoonDance Press, an imprint of The Quarto Group.
26391 Crown Valley Parkway, Suite 220, Mission Viejo, CA 92691, USA.
T (949) 380-7510 **F** (949) 380-7575 **www.QuartoKnows.com**

Walter Foster Publishing titles are also available at discount for retail, wholesale, promotional, and bulk purchase. For details, contact the Special Sales Manager by email at specialsales@quarto.com or by mail at The Quarto Group, Attn: Special Sales Manager, 100 Cummings Center, Suite 265D, Beverly, MA 01915, USA.

ISBN: 978-1-63322-150-5

Digital edition published in 2017
eISBN: 978-1-63322-433-9

Cover design and layout by Melissa Gerber

Printed in Guangdong, China
10 9 8 7 6 5 4 3 2 1
November 2019
19090228

Contents

Introduction

Listener up there! Here you.... what have you to confide to me?
Look in my face while I snuff the sidle of evening,
Talk honestly, for no one else hears you, and I stay only a minute longer.

Walt Whitman wants to speak with you—yes, you! What's more, he wants to listen to you too. "How can a book communicate so directly with me?" you might wonder as you wander through the freely flowing poems of *Leaves of Grass*. "This is no book," Walt answers from another page. "Who touches this touches a man."

Walt started a revolution in American cultural history by breaking all the rules. He got personal with his readers instead of maintaining a "safe" distance across the pages. He liberated poetry from traditional rhyme and meter, writing in long lines that sound—and even look—natural and free. He celebrated people and experiences that weren't considered proper subjects for literature, and preached equality across gender, race, and class. And he believed in poetry's power to change the world.

Walt is now recognized as America's greatest poet, and his collection of poetry entitled *Leaves of Grass* is considered America's cultural Declaration of Independence, second only to our political Declaration of 1776. But in many ways he is the least likely candidate for this title and honor. The story of Walt's journey as an artist is just about as exciting as his work, so the poems in this book have been carefully selected to guide you through his unconventional and extraordinary career.

This book's first section, "Starting From Paumanok," includes poems that focus on Walt's earliest years and his development as a poet. You will meet him on the beaches of his beloved "Paumanok" (the Algonquin tribe's name for Long Island), be there when he learns his poetic gift was inspired by nature, not school ("Out of the Cradle Endlessly Rocking"), and travel with him to Brooklyn, where he discovered his deep love for humanity ("Crossing Brooklyn Ferry").

"Walt Whitman, a Kosmos, of Manhattan the Son" is named after one of the most famous lines in "Song of Myself," Walt's great personal epic. These selections were written in his artistic prime, when he proclaimed himself and his work an independent universe or "kosmos." At the center of it all for Walt was New York City, and these poems reflect its influence.

The section entitled "The Wound-Dresser" includes Walt's greatest Civil War poems. In the title poem and other selections, you'll find that he wasn't just an onlooker or commentator on the war, but volunteered countless hours as a nurse and letter-writer for wounded soldiers.

"The Good Gray Poet" was a popular nickname for Walt in his later years. These poems present a man who has gained much in his life, including fearlessness of death. Though he did not receive the recognition he wanted, he welcomes you to fulfill his promise: "Leaving it to you to prove and define it,/ Expecting the main things from you" ("Poets to Come").

Walt and I both hope that, as you "listeners" look down into this book's "face," you'll find messages just for you. And as Whitman's life and work are revealed on the following pages, perhaps you'll be compelled to respond to him as so many others have. You may just find that you, too, have poetry inside of you.

Walt's Welcome

Song of the Open Road (excerpt)

Camerado, I give you my hand!
I give you my love more precious than money,
I give you myself before preaching or law;
Will you give me yourself? Will you come travel with me?
Shall we stick by each other as long as we live?

Camerado: Walt's own term for a true and loyal friend, probably influenced by the term "camaraderie" (mutual trust and friendship) or "camarade" (a French word for friend)

Starting From Paumanok

There Was A Child Went Forth (two excerpts)

There was a child went forth every day,
And the first object he looked upon and received with wonder or pity or love or dread, that object
    he became,
And that object became part of him for the day or a certain part of the day . . . . or
    for many years or stretching cycles of years.

The early lilacs became part of this child,
And grass, and white and red morningglories, and white and red clover, and the song of the
    phoebe-bird,
And the March-born lambs, and the sow's pink-faint litter, and the mare's foal, and
    the cow's calf, and the noisy brood of the barnyard or by the mire of the pond-
    side . . and the fish suspending themselves so curiously below there . . and the
    beautiful curious liquid . . and the water-plants with their graceful flat heads . . .

—◆—

These became part of that child who went forth every day, and who now goes and
    will always go forth every day,
And these become of him or her that peruses them now.

Mire: swampy ground
Peruses: observes

8

Paumanok

Sea-beauty! stretch'd and basking!
One side thy inland ocean laving, broad, with copious commerce, steamers, sails,
And one the Atlantic's wind caressing, fierce or gentle—mighty hulls dark-gliding in the
   distance.
Isle of sweet brooks of drinking-water—healthy air and soil!
Isle of the salty shore and breeze and brine!

Laving: flowing
Copious: abundant
Brine: salty water

The Sleepers (excerpt)

Now I tell what my mother told me today as we sat at dinner together,
Of when she was a nearly grown girl living home with her parents on the old homestead.

A red squaw came one breakfasttime to the old homestead,
On her back she carried a bundle of rushes for rushbottoming chairs;
Her hair straight shiny coarse black and profuse halfenveloped her face,
Her step was free and elastic . . . . her voice sounded exquisitely as she spoke.
My mother looked in delight and amazement at the stranger,
She looked at the beauty of her tallborne face and full and pliant limbs,
The more she looked upon her she loved her,
Never before had she seen such wonderful beauty and purity;
She made her sit on a bench by the jamb of the fireplace . . . . she cooked food for her,
She had no work to give her but she gave her remembrance and fondness.

The red squaw staid all the forenoon, and toward the middle of the afternoon she went away;
O my mother was loth to have her go away,
All the week she thought of her . . . . she watched for her many a month,
She remembered her many a winter and many a summer,
But the red squaw never came nor was heard of there again.

Squaw: a Native American woman
Rushbottoming: having a seat made with long grasses
Exquisitely: in a very fine and beautiful manner
Tallborne: Walt's word for "long," with a feeling of nobility borrowed from the word "highborn"
Jamb: side post

Out of the Cradle Endlessly Rocking (two excerpts)

Once, Paumanok,
When the snows had melted, and the Fifth Month grass was growing,
Up this sea-shore, in some briers,
Two guests from Alabama—two together,
And their nest, and four light-green eggs, spotted with brown,
And every day the he-bird, to and fro, near at hand,
And every day the she-bird, crouched on her nest, silent, with bright eyes,
And every day I, a curious boy, never too close, never disturbing them,
Cautiously peering, absorbing, translating.

Shine! Shine!
Pour down your warmth, great Sun!
While we bask—we two together.

Two together!
Winds blow South, or winds blow North,
Day come white, or night come black,
Home, or rivers and mountains from home,
Singing all time, minding no time,
If we two but keep together.

———◆———

Bird! (then said the boy's Soul,)
Is it indeed toward your mate you sing? or is it mostly to me?
For I that was a child, my tongue's use sleeping,
Now that I have heard you,
Now in a moment I know what I am for—I awake,
And already a thousand singers—a thousand songs, clearer, louder, more sorrowful than yours,
A thousand warbling echoes have started to life within me,
Never to die.

Fifth Month: the Quaker version of the month of May
Briers: prickly plants

Beginning My Studies

Beginning my studies the first step pleas'd me so much,
The mere fact consciousness, these forms, the power of motion,
The least insect or animal, the senses, eyesight, love,
The first step I say awed me and pleas'd me so much,
I have hardly gone and hardly wish'd to go any farther,
But stop and loiter all the time to sing it in ecstatic songs.

Loiter: linger
Ecstatic: full of joy

When I Heard the Learn'd Astronomer

When I heard the learn'd astronomer;
When the proofs, the figures, were ranged in columns before me;
When I was shown the charts and the diagrams, to add, divide, and measure them;
When I, sitting, heard the astronomer, where he lectured with much applause in the lecture-room,
How soon, unaccountable, I became tired and sick;
Till rising and gliding out, I wander'd off by myself,
In the mystical moist night-air, and from time to time,
Look'd up in perfect silence at the stars.

Unaccountable: without an explanation

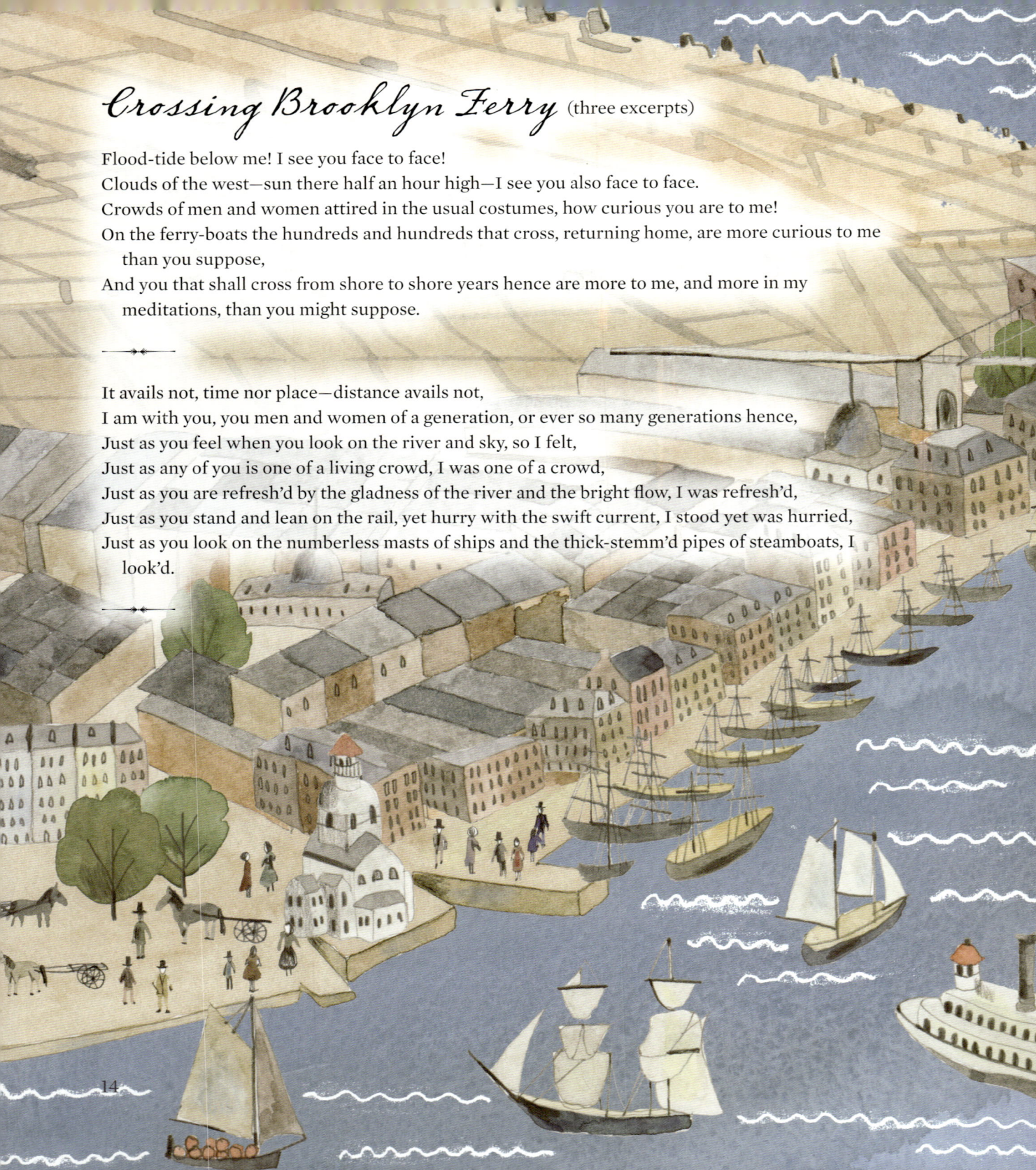

Crossing Brooklyn Ferry (three excerpts)

Flood-tide below me! I see you face to face!
Clouds of the west—sun there half an hour high—I see you also face to face.
Crowds of men and women attired in the usual costumes, how curious you are to me!
On the ferry-boats the hundreds and hundreds that cross, returning home, are more curious to me
than you suppose,
And you that shall cross from shore to shore years hence are more to me, and more in my
meditations, than you might suppose.

It avails not, time nor place—distance avails not,
I am with you, you men and women of a generation, or ever so many generations hence,
Just as you feel when you look on the river and sky, so I felt,
Just as any of you is one of a living crowd, I was one of a crowd,
Just as you are refresh'd by the gladness of the river and the bright flow, I was refresh'd,
Just as you stand and lean on the rail, yet hurry with the swift current, I stood yet was hurried,
Just as you look on the numberless masts of ships and the thick-stemm'd pipes of steamboats, I
look'd.

What is it then between us?
What is the count of the scores or hundreds of years between us?

Whatever it is, it avails not—distance avails not, and place avails not,
I too lived, Brooklyn of ample hills was mine,
I too walk'd the streets of Manhattan island, and bathed in the waters around it,
I too felt the curious abrupt questionings stir within me,
In the day among crowds of people sometimes they came upon me,
In my walks home late at night or as I lay in my bed they came upon me.

Hence: in the future
Avails: helps or benefits

15

A Font of Type

This latent mine—these unlaunch'd voices—passionate powers,
Wrath, argument, or praise, or comic leer, or prayer devout,
(Not nonpareil, brevier, bourgeois, long primer merely,)
These ocean waves arousable to fury and to death,
Or sooth'd to ease and sheeny sun and sleep,
Within the pallid slivers slumbering.

Latent: hidden
Unlaunch'd: not yet set free
Leer: glance
Nonpareil, brevier, bourgeois, long primer: sizes
  of type, from smallest to largest
Pallid: pale-colored, like a sheet of paper (Whitman's "slivers")

16

Walt Whitman, a Kosmos, of Manhattan the Son

Walt Whitman's Caution

To The States, or any one of them, or any city of The States, *Resist much, obey little*;
Once unquestioning obedience, once fully enslaved;
Once fully enslaved, no nation, state, city, of this earth, ever afterward resumes its liberty.

I Sing the Body Electric (excerpt)

A man's body at auction!
I help the auctioneer—the sloven does not half know his business.

Gentlemen, look on this wonder!
Whatever the bids of the bidders, they cannot be high enough for it,
For it the globe lay preparing quintillions of years, without one animal or plant,
For it the revolving cycles truly and steadily rolled.

In this head the all-baffling brain,
In it and below it the making of the attributes of heroes.

Examine these limbs, red, black, or white—they are so cunning in tendon and nerve,
They shall be stript that you may see them.

Exquisite senses, life-lit eyes, pluck, volition,
Flakes of breast-muscle, pliant back-bone and neck, flesh not flabby, good-sized arms and legs,
And wonders within there yet.

Within there runs blood—the same old blood! the same red running blood!
There swells and jets a heart—there all passions, desires, reachings, aspirations,
Do you think they are not there because they are not expressed in parlors and lecture-rooms?

This is not only one man—this is the father of those who shall be fathers in their turns,
In him the start of populous states and rich republics,
Of him countless immortal lives, with countless embodiments and enjoyments.

How do you know who shall come from the offspring of his offspring through the centuries?
Who might you find you have come from yourself, if you could trace back through the centuries?

Sloven: careless, vulgar person
All-baffling: Walt's word for "mystifying everyone"
Pluck: spirited courage
Volition: the power to make one's own choices

A Woman Waits for Me (excerpt)

They are not one jot less than I am,
They are tann'd in the face by shining suns and blowing winds,
Their flesh has the old divine suppleness and strength,
They know how to swim, row, ride, wrestle, shoot, run, strike, retreat, advance, resist, defend themselves,
They are ultimate in their own right—they are calm, clear, well-possess'd of themselves.

Jot: bit (Walt is thinking of tiny drips from his pen)
Suppleness: flexibility

City of Ships (excerpt)

City of the world! (for all races are here;
All the lands of the earth make contributions here;)
City of the sea! city of hurried and glittering tides!
City whose gleeful tides continually rush or recede, whirling in and out, with eddies and foam!
City of wharves and stores! city of tall façades of marble and iron!
Proud and passionate city! mettlesome, mad, extravagant city!

Eddies: currents of water
Façades: building fronts
Mettlesome: spirited
Mad: crazy

20

Give Me the Splendid Silent Sun

1.

Give me the splendid silent sun, with all his beams full-dazzling;

Give me juicy autumnal fruit, ripe and red from the orchard;

Give me a field where the unmow'd grass grows;

Give me an arbor, give me the trellis'd grape;

Give me fresh corn and wheat—give me serene-moving animals, teaching content;

Give me nights perfectly quiet, as on high plateaus west of the Mississippi, and I looking up at the stars;

Give me odorous at sunrise a garden of beautiful flowers, where I can walk undisturb'd;

Give me for marriage a sweet-breath'd woman, of whom I should never tire;

Give me a perfect child—give me, away, aside from the noise of the world, a rural domestic life;

Give me to warble spontaneous songs, reliev'd, recluse by myself, for my own ears only;

Give me solitude—give me Nature—give me again,

O Nature, your primal sanities!

—These, demanding to have them, (tired with ceaseless excitement, and rack'd by the war-strife;)

These to procure, incessantly asking, rising in cries from my heart,

While yet incessantly asking, still I adhere to my city;

Day upon day, and year upon year, O city, walking your streets,

Where you hold me enchain'd a certain time, refusing to give me up;

Yet giving to make me glutted, enrich'd of soul—you give me forever faces;

(O I see what I sought to escape, confronting, reversing my cries;

I see my own soul trampling down what it ask'd for.)

Recluse: alone
Primal sanities: basic sources of
    contentment and joy
Procure: find
Incessantly: constantly
Glutted: overfull
Phantoms incessant: constant parade
    of spirits
Troittoirs: sidewalks
Interminable: endless
Wharves: docks
Repletion: overfullness
Brigade: large body of army troops

2.

Keep your splendid silent sun;
Keep your woods, O Nature, and the quiet places by the woods;
Keep your fields of clover and timothy, and your cornfields and orchards;
Keep the blossoming buckwheat fields, where the Ninth-month bees hum;
Give me faces and streets! give me these phantoms incessant and endless along the trottoirs!
Give me interminable eyes! give me women! give me comrades and lovers by the thousand!
Let me see new ones every day! let me hold new ones by the hand every day!
Give me such shows! give me the streets of Manhattan!
Give me Broadway, with the soldiers marching—give me the sound of the trumpets and drums!
(The soldiers in companies or regiments—some, starting away, flush'd and reckless;
Some, their time up, returning, with thinn'd ranks—young, yet very old, worn, marching, noticing nothing;)
—Give me the shores and the wharves heavy-fringed with the black ships!
O such for me! O an intense life! O full to repletion, and varied!
The life of the theatre, bar-room, huge hotel, for me!
The saloon of the steamer! the crowded excursion for me! the torch-light procession!
The dense brigade, bound for the war, with high piled military wagons following;
People, endless, streaming, with strong voices, passions, pageants;
Manhattan streets, with their powerful throbs, with the beating drums, as now; The endless and noisy chorus, the rustle and clank of muskets, (even the sight of the wounded;)
Manhattan crowds with their turbulent musical chorus—with varied chorus and light of the sparkling eyes;
Manhattan faces and eyes forever for me.

Song of Myself

(FIRST EXCERPT)

I celebrate myself,
And what I assume you shall assume,
For every atom belonging to me as good belongs to you.

I loafe and invite my soul,
I lean and loafe at my ease . . . . observing a spear of summer grass.

Loafe: laze about

(SECOND EXCERPT)

Have you reckoned a thousand acres much? Have you reckoned the earth much?
Have you practiced so long to learn to read?
Have you felt so proud to get at the meaning of poems?

Stop this day and night with me and you shall possess the origin of all poems,
You shall possess the good of the earth and sun . . . . there are millions of suns left,
You shall no longer take things at second or third hand . . . . nor look through the eyes of the
    dead . . . . nor feed on the spectres in books,
You shall not look through my eyes either, nor take things from me,
You shall listen to all sides and filter them from yourself.

Reckoned: considered
Spectres: imagined apparitions

24

(THIRD EXCERPT)

Walt Whitman, a kosmos, of Manhattan the son,
Turbulent, fleshy, sensual, eating, drinking and breeding,
No sentimentalist, no stander above men and women or apart from them,
No more modest than immodest.

Unscrew the locks from the doors!
Unscrew the doors themselves from their jambs!

Kosmos: universe
Turbulent: not organized or orderly
Sentimentalist: someone who is more
emotional than sensible

I am of old and young, of the foolish as much as the wise,

Regardless of others, ever regardful of others,

Maternal as well as paternal, a child as well as a man,

Stuffed with the stuff that is coarse, and stuffed with the stuff that is fine,

One of the great nation, the nation of many nations—the smallest the same and the largest the same,

A southerner soon as a northerner, a planter nonchalant and hospitable,

A Yankee bound my own way . . . . ready for trade . . . . my joints the limberest joints on earth
and the sternest joints on earth,

A Kentuckian walking the vale of the Elkhorn in my deerskin leggings,

A boatman over the lakes or bays or along coasts . . . . a Hoosier, a Badger, a Buckeye,

A Louisianian or Georgian, a poke-easy from sandhills and pines,

At home on Canadian snowshoes or up in the bush, or with fishermen off Newfoundland,

At home in the fleet of iceboats, sailing with the rest and tacking,

At home on the hills of Vermont or in the woods of Maine or the Texan ranch,

Comrade of Californians . . . . comrade of free northwesterners, loving their big proportions,

Comrade of raftsmen and coalmen—comrade of all who shake hands and welcome to drink and meat;

A learner with the simplest, a teacher of the thoughtfulest,

A novice beginning experient of myriads of seasons,

Of every hue and trade and rank, of every caste and religion,

Not merely of the New World but of Africa Europe or Asia . . . . a wandering savage,

A farmer, mechanic, or artist . . . . a gentleman, sailor, lover or quaker,

A prisoner, fancy-man, rowdy, lawyer, physician or priest.

Nonchalant: relaxed
Sternest: firmest
Hoosier: person from Indiana
Badger: someone from Ohio
Poke-easy: easygoing person
Tacking: changing course
Beginning experient: starting to experience
Myriads: countless
Quaker: member of a Christian movement believing in a direct relationship with God
Fancy-man: a man who places particular importance on his appearance

Agonies are one of my changes of garments;
I do not ask the wounded person how he feels . . . . I myself become the wounded person,
My hurt turns livid upon me as I lean on a cane and observe.

I am the mashed fireman with breastbone broken . . . . tumbling walls buried me in their debris,
Heat and smoke I inspired . . . . I heard the yelling shouts of my comrades,
I heard the distant click of their picks and shovels;
They have cleared the beams away . . . . they tenderly lift me forth.

I lie in the night air in my red shirt . . . . the pervading hush is for my sake,
Painless after all I lie, exhausted but not so unhappy,
White and beautiful are the faces around me . . . . the heads are bared of their fire-caps,
The kneeling crowd fades with the light of the torches.

Livid: furiously
Debris: scattered fragments
Pervading: spreading

(SIXTH EXCERPT)

I depart as air . . . . I shake my white locks at the runaway sun,
I effuse my flesh in eddies and drift it in lacy jags.
I bequeath myself to the dirt to grow from the grass I love,
If you want me again look for me under your bootsoles.

You will hardly know who I am or what I mean,
But I shall be good health to you nevertheless,
And filter and fibre your blood.

Failing to fetch me at first keep encouraged,
Missing me one place search another,
I stop some where waiting for you

Effuse: to pour forth
Lacy jags: foamy ripples of water
Bequeath: leave or entrust to
Fibre: Walt's version of "fiber;" to add
  substance or to thicken

Shut Not Your Doors

Shut not your doors to me proud libraries,
For that which was lacking on all your well-fill'd shelves, yet needed most, I bring,
Forth from the war emerging, a book I have made,
The words of my book nothing, the drift of it every thing,
A book separate, not link'd with the rest nor felt by the intellect,
But you ye untold latencies will thrill to every page.

Drift: Walt's word for essence or gist, as
in the saying "get my drift?"
Latencies: hidden things

Calamus 9

Hours continuing long, sore and heavy-hearted,

Hours of the dusk, when I withdraw to a lonesome and unfrequented spot, seating myself,
   leaning my face in my hands;

Hours sleepless, deep in the night, when I go forth, speeding swiftly the country roads, or
   through the city streets, or pacing miles and miles, stifling plaintive cries;

Hours discouraged, distracted—for the one I cannot content myself without, soon I saw him
   content himself without me;

Hours when I am forgotten, (O weeks and months are passing, but I believe I am never to forget!)

Sullen and suffering hours! (I am ashamed—but it is useless—I am what I am;)

Hours of my torment—I wonder if other men ever have the like, out of the like feelings?

Is there even one other like me—distracted—his friend, his lover, lost to him?

Is he too as I am now? Does he still rise in the morning, dejected, thinking who is lost to him?
   and at night, awaking, think who is lost?

Does he too harbor his friendship silent and endless? harbor his anguish and passion?

Does some stray reminder, or the casual mention of a name, bring the fit back upon him, taciturn
   and deprest?

Does he see himself reflected in me? In these hours, does he see the face of his hours reflected?

Stifling: holding back
Plaintive: mournful
Taciturn: uncommunicative
Deprest: Walt's version of "depressed"

The Wound-Dresser

Beat! Beat! Drums!

1

Beat! beat! drums!—Blow! bugles! blow!
Through the windows—through doors—burst like a force of ruthless men,
Into the solemn church, and scatter the congregation;
Into the school where the scholar is studying:
Leave not the bridegroom quiet—no happiness must he have now with his bride;
Nor the peaceful farmer any peace, plowing his field or gathering his grain;
So fierce you whirr and pound, you drums—so shrill you bugles blow.

2

Beat! beat! drums!—Blow! bugles! blow!
Over the traffic of cities—over the rumble of wheels in the streets:
Are beds prepared for sleepers at night in the houses?
No sleepers must sleep in those beds;
No bargainers' bargains by day—no brokers or speculators —Would they continue?
Would the talkers be talking? would the singer attempt to sing?
Would the lawyer rise in the court to state his case before the judge?
Then rattle quicker, heavier drums—you bugles wilder blow.

3

Beat! beat! drums!—Blow! bugles! blow!
Make no parley—stop for no expostulation;
Mind not the timid—mind not the weeper or prayer;
Mind not the old man beseeching the young man;
Let not the child's voice be heard, nor the mother's entreaties;
Make even the trestles to shake the dead, where they lie awaiting the hearses,
So strong you thump, O terrible drums—so loud you bugles blow.

Brokers or speculators: onlookers who do not actively engage in the scene,
*   but make money from making bets or taking sides*
Parley: negotiation
Expostulation: protest
Trestles: supporting beams
Hearses: vehicles carrying coffins at funerals

The Wound-Dresser (excerpt)

I dress a wound in the side, deep, deep,
But a day or two more, for see the frame all wasted and sinking,
And the yellow-blue countenance see.

I dress the perforated shoulder, the foot with the bullet-wound,
Cleanse the one with a gnawing and putrid gangrene, so sickening, so offensive,
While the attendant stands behind aside me holding the tray and pail.

I am faithful, I do not give out,
The fractur'd thigh, the knee, the wound in the abdomen,
These and more I dress with impassive hand, (yet deep in my
    breast a fire, a burning flame.)

Frame: body
Countenance: a person's face
Perforated: pierced
Gangrene: decomposition of body tissue because of infection or blocked blood flow
Impassive: not showing emotion

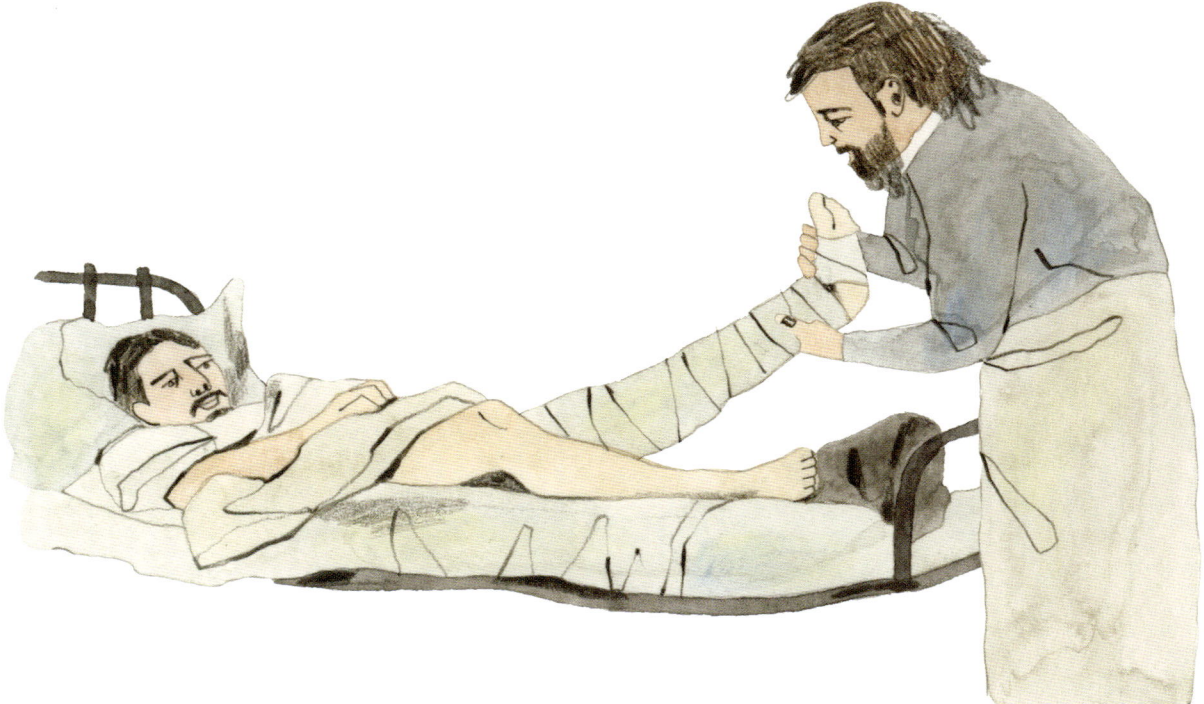

33

Come Up From the Fields Father

Come up from the fields, father, here's a letter from our Pete;
And come to the front door, mother—here's a letter from thy dear son.

Lo, 'tis autumn;
Lo, where the trees, deeper green, yellower and redder,
Cool and sweeten Ohio's villages, with leaves fluttering in the moderate wind;
Where apples ripe in the orchards hang, and grapes on the trellis'd vines;
(Smell you the smell of the grapes on the vines?
Smell you the buckwheat, where the bees were lately buzzing?)

Above all, lo, the sky, so calm, so transparent after the rain, and with wondrous clouds;
Below, too, all calm, all vital and beautiful—and the farm prospers well.

Down in the fields all prospers well;
But now from the fields come, father—come at the daughter's call;
And come to the entry, mother—to the front door come, right away.

Fast as she can she hurries—something ominous— her steps trembling;
She does not tarry to smooth her white hair, nor adjust her cap.

Open the envelope quickly;
O this is not our son's writing, yet his name is sign'd;
O a strange hand writes for our dear son—O stricken mother's soul!
All swims before her eyes—flashes with black—she catches the main words only;
Sentences broken—*gun-shot wound in the breast, cavalry skirmish, taken to hospital,*
At present low, but will soon be better.

Ah, now the single figure to me,
Amid all teeming and wealthy Ohio, with all its cities and farms,
Sickly white in the face and dull in the head, very faint,

By the jamb of a door leans.

Grieve not so, dear mother, (the just-grown daughter speaks through her sobs;
The little sisters huddle around, speechless and dismay'd;)
See, dearest mother, the letter says Pete will soon be better.

Alas, poor boy, he will never be better, (nor may-be needs to be better, that brave and simple soul;)
While they stand at home at the door, he is dead already;
The only son is dead.

But the mother needs to be better;
She, with thin form, presently drest in black;
By day her meals untouch'd—then at night fitfully sleeping, often waking,
In the midnight waking, weeping, longing with one deep longing,
O that she might withdraw unnoticed—silent from life, escape and withdraw,
To follow, to seek, to be with her dear dead son.

Tarry: delay
Teeming: bustling, busy
Dismay'd: distressed

As Toilsome I Wander'd Virginia's Woods

As toilsome I wander'd Virginia's woods,
To the music of rustling leaves kick'd by my feet, (for 'twas autumn,)
   I mark'd at the foot of a tree the grave of a soldier;
Mortally wounded he and buried on the retreat, (easily all could I understand,)
The halt of a mid-day hour, when up! no time to lose—yet this sign left,
On a tablet scrawl'd and nail'd on the tree by the grave,
Bold, cautious, true, and my loving comrade.

Long, long I muse, then on my way go wandering,
Many a changeful season to follow, and many a scene of life,
Yet at times through changeful season and scene, abrupt, alone,
   or in the crowded street,
Comes before me the unknown soldier's grave, comes the inscrip-
   tion rude in Virginia's woods,
Bold, cautious, true, and my loving comrade.

Toilsome: wearily
Mark'd: Walt's version of "marked," or "noted"

36

O Captain! My Captain!

O Captain! my Captain! our fearful trip is done,
The ship has weather'd every rack, the prize we sought is won,
The port is near, the bells I hear, the people all exulting,
While follow eyes the steady keel, the vessel grim and daring;
  But O heart! heart! heart!
   O the bleeding drops of red,
    Where on the deck my Captain lies,
     Fallen cold and dead.

O Captain! my Captain! rise up and hear the bells;
Rise up—for you the flag is flung—for you the bugle trills,
For you bouquets and ribbon'd wreaths—for you the shores
    a-crowding,
For you they call, the swaying mass, their eager faces turning;
  Here Captain! dear father!
   This arm beneath your head!
    It is some dream that on the deck,
     You've fallen cold and dead.

My Captain does not answer, his lips are pale and still,
My father does not feel my arm, he has no pulse nor will,
The ship is anchor'd safe and sound, its voyage closed and
    done,
From fearful trip the victor ship comes in with object won;
  Exult O shores, and ring O bells!
   But I with mournful tread,
    Walk the deck my Captain lies,
     Fallen cold and dead.

Rack: hard blow
Exulting: rejoicing
Keel: a lengthwise structure along the
  bottom of a boat that provides stability
Tread: steps

Aboard at a Ship's Helm

Aboard, at the ship's helm,
A young steersman, steering with care.

A bell through fog on a sea-coast dolefully ringing,
An ocean-bell—O a warning bell, rock'd by the waves.

O you give good notice indeed, you bell by the sea-reefs ringing,
Ringing, ringing, to warn the ship from its wreck-place.

For, as on the alert, O steersman, you mind the bell's admonition,
The bows turn,—the freighted ship, tacking, speeds away under her
    gray sails,
The beautiful and noble ship, with all her precious wealth, speeds
    away gaily and safe.

But O the ship, the immortal ship! O ship aboard the ship!
O ship of the body—ship of the soul—voyaging, voyaging, voyaging.

Helm: *steering gear of a ship*
Dolefully: *gloomily*

The Good Gray Poet

O Me! O Life!

O me! O life! of the questions of these recurring,
Of the endless trains of the faithless, of cities fill'd with the foolish,
Of myself forever reproaching myself, (for who more foolish than I, and who more
  faithless?)
Of eyes that vainly crave the light, of the objects mean, of the struggle ever renew'd,
Of the poor results of all, of the plodding and sordid crowds I see around me,
Of the empty and useless years of the rest, with the rest me intertwined,
The question, O me! so sad, recurring—What good amid these, O me, O life?
Answer.
That you are here—that life exists and identity,
That the powerful play goes on, and you may contribute a verse.

Plodding: slow-moving, unexciting
Sordid: dishonorable

On the Beach at Night

On the beach at night,
Stands a child with her father,
Watching the east, the autumn sky.

Up through the darkness,
While ravening clouds, the burial clouds, in black masses spreading,
Lower sullen and fast athwart and down the sky,
Amid a transparent clear belt of ether yet left in the east,
Ascends large and calm the lord-star Jupiter,
And nigh at hand, only a very little above,
Swim the delicate sisters the Pleiades.

From the beach the child holding the hand of her father,
Those burial-clouds that lower victorious soon to devour all,
Watching, silently weeps.

Weep not, child,
Weep not, my darling,
With these kisses let me remove your tears,
The ravening clouds shall not long be victorious,

They shall not long possess the sky, they devour the stars only in apparition,
Jupiter shall emerge, be patient, watch again another night, the Pleiades shall emerge,
They are immortal, all those stars both silvery and golden shall shine out again,
The great stars and the little ones shall shine out again, they endure,
The vast immortal suns and the long-enduring pensive moons shall again shine.

Then dearest child mournest thou only for Jupiter?
Considerest thou alone the burial of the stars?

Something there is,
(With my lips soothing thee, adding I whisper,
I give thee the first suggestion, the problem and indirection,)
Something there is more immortal even than the stars,
(Many the burials, many the days and nights, passing away,)
Something that shall endure longer even than lustrous Jupiter,
Longer than sun or any revolving satellite,
Or the radiant sisters the Pleiades.

Athwart: across
Ether: clear sky; upper regions of air beyond
  the clouds
Nigh: near
Burial-clouds: clouds that cover—and seem
  to bury—the stars
Ravening: very hungry and hunting for prey
Apparition: illusion
Lustrous: radiant
Revolving satellite: a rotating celestial body,
  such as Earth's moon

A Noiseless Patient Spider

A noiseless patient spider,
I mark'd where on a little promontory it stood isolated,
Mark'd how to explore the vacant vast surrounding,
It launch'd forth filament, filament, filament, out of itself,
Ever unreeling them, ever tirelessly speeding them.

And you O my soul where you stand,
Surrounded, detached, in measureless oceans of space,
Ceaselessly musing, venturing, throwing, seeking the spheres to connect them,
Till the bridge you will need be form'd, till the ductile anchor hold,
Till the gossamer thread you fling catch somewhere, O my soul.

Promontory: high point
Vacant: open and free
Filament: a slender thread
Ductile: stretchable yet strong
Gossamer: fine and filmy, as in a thread
 from a cobweb

Thanks in Old Age

Thanks in old age—thanks ere I go,

For health, the midday sun, the impalpable air—for life, mere life,

For precious ever-lingering memories, (of you my mother dear—you, father—you, brothers, sisters, friends,)

For all my days—not those of peace alone—the days of war the same,

For gentle words, caresses, gifts from foreign lands,

For shelter, wine and meat—for sweet appreciation,

(You distant, dim unknown—or young or old—countless, unspecified, readers belov'd,

We never met, and ne'er shall meet—and yet our souls embrace, long, close and long;)

For beings, groups, love, deeds, words, books—for colors, forms,

For all the brave strong men—devoted, hardy men—who've forward sprung in freedom's help, all years, all lands,

For braver, stronger, more devoted men—(a special laurel ere I go, to life's war's chosen ones,

The cannoneers of song and thought—the great artillerists—the foremost leaders, captains of the soul:)

As soldier from an ended war return'd—As traveler out of myriads, to the long procession retrospective,

Thanks—joyful thanks!—a soldier's, traveler's thanks.

Ere: *before*
Impalpable: *not easily understood or felt*
Laurel: *honor*
Cannoneers: *here, Walt means "soldiers" in the "war" known as life*
Artillerists: *more "service people" of "life's war"*
Myriads: *countless numbers*
Procession retrospective: *a 'parade of the past.' Nearing the end of his life's travels, Walt is envisioning his past experiences marching before him.*

43

Poets to Come

Poets to come! orators, singers, musicians to come!
Not to-day is to justify me and answer what I am for,
But you, a new brood, native, athletic, continental, greater than before known,
Arouse! for you must justify me.

I myself but write one or two indicative words for the future,
I but advance a moment only to wheel and hurry back in the darkness.

I am a man who, sauntering along without fully stopping, turns a casual look upon you and then
    averts his face,
Leaving it to you to prove and define it,
Expecting the main things from you.

Continental: characteristic of a continent; here, Walt means "expansive"
Indicative: representative
Sauntering: strolling

What Walt Was Thinking

Song of the Open Road **(1892):** Here, at the start of our journey through Whitman's life and work, Walt urges you to join him on the open road. He asks you to leave behind your papers, books, and doubts, and instead take his hand and experience the adventure of your lifetime.

There Was a Child Went Forth **(1855):** Walt believed experiences form our characters, from our earliest interactions with the world to what we're doing right now. Here, he explores this idea in which he recalls seemingly unimportant memories of his childhood on a Long Island farm — experiences that helped to make him the poet he became.

Paumanok **(1892):** Published near the end of his life, this poem demonstrates Walt's enduring affection for his birthplace: Long Island. He preferred to call it "Paumanok" as a tribute to the island's Native American roots. His love of sea imagery in his poems is rooted in his early years exploring Long Island's beaches.

The Sleepers **(1855):** The poet here recalls a tale of his mother's aborted friendship with a local squaw. Long Island's indigenous population would be nearly obliterated during Walt's own lifetime, and his mother's personal loss in the story echoes the new country's disconnection from its aboriginal roots.

Out of the Cradle Endlessly Rocking **(1860):** In the first excerpt, Walt claims that his poetic gift was not given to him by teachers or even his family, but by nature. In the second excerpt, the boy is overcome with joy when he realizes that he can understand the birds — and then devastated to learn that one of them never returns to his mate. He then listens to the tragic song of the he-bird ... and realizes that he has discovered his own poetic voice.

Beginning My Studies **(1892):** As a teacher in his late teens and early 20s, Whitman used what were considered progressive techniques — such as encouraging students to discuss rather than simply memorize and recite and inventing educational games. In this poem, we meet one of his ideal pupils: someone who might not like lessons or lectures, but obviously loves to learn.

When I Heard the Learn'd Astronomer **(1865):** Walt went to Brooklyn's first public school but wasn't the type to benefit from a traditional education. This poem hints at why: Walt would rather look at the universe with the naked eye rather than the most sophisticated calibrated telescope. Science is a noble pursuit that is necessary to sustain and better our lives; poetry is what we stay alive for.

Crossing Brooklyn Ferry **(1892):** When Walt was four years old, his father moved the growing Whitman family from their farm to the bustling city of Brooklyn. Although Walt always cherished a connection with nature, he quickly fell in love with urban life. In this much-loved poem, the narrator connects with us future readers by thinking about how we, too, will be fascinated by this colorful and ever-moving cityscape.

A Font of Type **(1892):** Walt had to drop out of school at age eleven to help support his seven siblings. First working for a lawyer, he eventually found work in a printing office. It was a lucky accident: Printing is the only working class profession in which being able to read is an important skill. This poem celebrates what to most folks looks like an ordinary typewritten page, but to Walt is a gorgeous sea of possibility.

***Walt Whitman's Caution* (1860):** By age 27, Walt had worked his way up to the position of editor of the *Brooklyn Daily Eagle*, an important newspaper. This helped Walt shape and define his politics, which grew more radical through the 1840s and '50s. He was fired after less than two years for his anti-slavery beliefs. This poem contains a line that might have irritated some of his employers, but has become a favorite of his readers.

***I Sing the Body Electric* (1856):** When Walt visited New Orleans in his 28th year, he witnessed his first slave auction in a public square. The experience had a strong effect on his feelings about racism and abolition, as can be seen from this excerpt from a poem first titled "Poem of a Black Person." He "helps" the slave auctioneer by drawing attention to the pricelessness of the slave — who has the same qualities and potential as the rest of humankind, including the auctioneer himself.

***A Woman Waits for Me* (1860):** Women's rights and abolitionism were two revolutionary movements that developed simultaneously in the mid-nineteenth century. In his journalism, Walt had long defended women's rights for fair salaries and equal treatment. This poem celebrates their strength of character as well as their physical bodies. His ideas were considered so progressive that this poem was banned from publication in 1882.

***City of Ships* (1865):** Manhattan was a microcosm of the world to Walt. Its energy and spectacular show of progress and ambition inspired him to his own form of greatness.

***Give Me the Splendid Silent Sun* (1865):** Walt's trip to the Midwest and the South in 1848 gave him his first experience of the rest of America beyond New York. In the first part of the poem, Walt celebrates the people, scenes, and more relaxed lifestyle that he encountered while on the road. In the second part, Walt takes back everything he just said and bares his city soul. He fell in love with New York at a time when other writers simply did not find inspiration or even a reason to live in the city. Walt felt energized instead of overwhelmed by its constant motion, heard music instead of madness in its street din, and saw humanity instead of strangeness in its crowds.

***Song of Myself, first excerpt* (1855):** From the very first lines of the first poem in *Leaves of Grass*, we readers are invited to a new way of thinking — about the purpose of poetry, our relationship with our poets, and the "United" idea of the States. We start by reconsidering the grass that we often simply stroll over. As the most democratic of plants, grass represents America: Each leaf is important to the idea of the whole.

***Song of Myself, second excerpt* (1855):** Walt conceived of *Leaves of Grass* as America's cultural Declaration of Independence. This document, like the original written by the Founding Fathers, promises a new beginning, new freedoms ... a New World.

***Song of Myself, third excerpt* (1892):** The collection of poems entitled *Leaves of Grass* was the product of a fiercely independent spirit. No publisher was willing to risk his reputation on twelve radical poems written by a relative nobody, so Walt designed the book himself, printing and publishing it with the help of Brooklyn friends and neighbors.

***Song of Myself, fourth excerpt* (1855):** Walt hoped to provide a vivid, sweeping image of America in such catalogs as this one. Can you find yourself in it?

***Song of Myself, fifth excerpt* (1855):** As a journalist, Whitman "became" his subjects in order to better understand and connect with them. These lines are surely inspired by his reporting of New York's great fires in the 1840s.

***Song of Myself, sixth excerpt* (1855):** Walt's struggle to keep the conversation going with us readers is evident near the end of "Song of Myself," the longest and best-known poem in *Leaves of Grass*. He makes it clear that he is present — in the air, in our water, in the ground beneath our feet. Besides the meaning of his words, the typesetting of these famous last lines, particularly the missing final period, suggest that he is indeed waiting somewhere for us.

Shut Not Your Doors (1892): Walt never achieved the success he imagined for his poetic experiment, *Leaves of Grass*. Here, he defies the many critics of his unusual writing style and subjects, and dares readers to appreciate his book's individuality and innovations.

Calamus 9 (1860): While America's struggle with the issue of slavery resulted in a major political crisis, Whitman's desire to love and be loved brought about his own profound emotional crisis. Perhaps his most personal poem is "Calamus 9," in which the poet asks difficult questions about his identity and wonders if anyone else is suffering because of similar feelings and doubts. The poem ends with questions that reach out to us. Many have found in this poem the brave voice of a person who tried to express himself freely — not just who he was, but whom he chose to love.

Beat! Beat! Drums! (1865): On April 12, 1861, Whitman read about the first shots fired at Fort Sumter, South Carolina. The Civil War had begun. This popular poem conveys Whitman's initial excitement about the prospect of fighting in the name of justice, equality, and union.

The Wound-Dresser (1892): Too old to take part in the fighting, Walt volunteered in the makeshift hospital tents that were scattered around Washington D.C., and thus was a firsthand witness to the war's aftermath. "The Wound-Dresser" provides graphic images of what Whitman must have seen in over two years of service to the solders. It also hints at his suppressed anger regarding the terrible casualties of the Civil War.

Come Up From the Fields Father (1865): From early 1863 to the end of the Civil War in the spring of 1865, Walt visited army hospitals daily and wrote hundreds of letters that briefed families on soldiers' conditions. It was his way of connecting Americans during a war that threatened to tear the country apart. In this poem, Whitman the letter writer is a "silent" witness to one family tragedy, which represents so many others.

As Toilsome I Wander'd Virginia's Woods (1892): Part of Walt's mission as a poet was to make sure his country never forgot the great sacrifice it had made to achieve union. Many of his greatest poems of the Civil War seek to humanize the daunting numbers of the dead and to remind Americans that each of these victims deserves commemoration and respect.

O Captain! My Captain! (1892): On April 14, 1865, five days after the April 9th surrender of Confederate commanding general Robert E. Lee, President Abraham Lincoln was assassinated. Whitman had felt a special bond with Lincoln because of their shared humble roots and their position on slavery and abolition. The loss of the "Captain" of the Union's "ship" was thus also a personal one for Whitman, who describes Lincoln as "father." The poem isn't written in his typical style — note its regular rhyme and rhythm, and its use of a subject that is not Whitman, for a change — and yet it is one of his most popular works.

Aboard at a Ship's Helm (1867): Though the Union Army had won the war, Lincoln's assassination left the country's fate in doubt. Walt's poetry right after the war reflects these insecurities. Soon after composing "O Captain! My Captain!", Walt picked up on the ship imagery once again, this time placing a new and inexperienced captain at the helm.

O Me! O Life! (1892): The years leading up to the Civil War as well as the war itself were troubled times for Walt. The speaker of this poem asks a question about existence that expresses his frustration — and then courageously answers it, reminding us that we all have a role in the ongoing drama of life. What will your verse be?

On the Beach at Night (1867): Whitman's postwar questions and worries led to the composition of poems focused on the concept of immortality. Looking at the stars and planets while standing on the shore with her father, a young girl worries that they have disappeared forever behind the clouds. Her father comforts her by telling her that they will re-emerge and endure. She (and we) are left wondering: Is there really such a thing as death?

A Noiseless Patient Spider (1892): In this favorite poem, a tiny insect represents the depths of a human soul. This late composition also shows that Walt — who had built his career on being the poet of the "now" — was setting his sights on the future, as the spider cast his line into unknown space.

Thanks in Old Age (1892): Whitman had much to be thankful for by the time he died at age 72 on March 26, 1892. He had grown his *Leaves* through six different editions and from twelve to over 400 poems. He had served his country during the Civil War. He had many enduring friendships and had even had a great love in his life. Most importantly, he had been true to himself and his poetic vision. He never compromised and always followed his heart. In this poem, Whitman expresses gratitude for life's everyday joys.

Poets to Come (1892): The poets to come … are us! Walt reaches out beyond the confines of time and asks us to carry his message into the future. He has supplied the canvas and a few words of guidance, but we are to paint the masterpiece.

Index

THE POETRY COLLECTION

Robert Frost

THE POETRY COLLECTION

Robert Frost

EDITED BY JAY PARINI
ILLUSTRATED BY
MICHAEL PARASKEVAS

MoonDance

Brimming with creative inspiration, how-to projects, and useful information to enrich your everyday life, Quarto Knows is a favorite destination for those pursuing their interests and passions. Visit our site and dig deeper with our books into your area of interest: Quarto Creates, Quarto Cooks, Quarto Homes, Quarto Lives, Quarto Drives, Quarto Explores, Quarto Gifts, or Quarto Kids.

© 2018 Quarto Publishing Group USA Inc.
Original text © 2017 Jay Parini
Illustrations © 2017 Michael Paraskevas

First Published in 2017 by Published by MoonDance Press, an imprint of The Quarto Group.
26391 Crown Valley Parkway, Suite 220, Mission Viejo, CA 92691, USA.
T (949) 380-7510 **F** (949) 380-7575 **www.QuartoKnows.com**

Walter Foster Publishing titles are also available at discount for retail, wholesale, promotional, and bulk purchase. For details, contact the Special Sales Manager by email at specialsales@quarto.com or by mail at The Quarto Group, Attn: Special Sales Manager, 100 Cummings Center, Suite 265D, Beverly, MA 01915, USA.

ISBN: 978-1-63322-220-5

Digital edition published in 2017
eISBN: 978-1-63322-566-4

Cover design and layout by Melissa Gerber

Printed in Guangdong, China
10 9 8 7 6 5 4 3 2 1
November 2019
19090228

MIX
Paper from
responsible sources
FSC® C016973
FSC
www.fsc.org

Contents

Introduction

Robert Frost (1874–1963) once said that a poem should "begin in delight and end in wisdom." Frost's poems are both delightful—full of humor and high spirits—and wise. They often deliver a nugget of truth that stays with you long after you put the poem down.

Frost's poems are usually set in northern New England, especially in New Hampshire and Vermont, where he lived on farms throughout his long life. Unsurprisingly, his best poems deal with the everyday work of farm labor. They focus on such tasks as sowing seeds in the ground in springtime, mowing a hayfield at the end of summer, and picking apples in the fall.

Frost believed strongly in metaphor—that is, saying one thing in terms of another. For example, in the poem "Mowing," he uses the language of harvesting crops (describing mowing wheat and setting it in the sun to ripen) to talk about feelings and writing poetry. When the poet harvests the emotions of a time period, he cuts them down, bundles them into lines or stanzas, and allows the hay "to make." Almost any of the poems in this collection can be read as a metaphor. Frost writes simply about a task or a situation and invites you to think in wider terms about the image or idea that centers the poem.

Frost was born in San Francisco, California, and lived there with his parents and his sister until he was eleven years old, when his father died. He then moved with his family to Massachusetts, where he attended high school. After an early marriage and two attempts at college, he settled on a farm in Derry, New Hampshire. There he and his wife, Elinor, raised chickens and four young children.

Frost loved going to the general store in town, where he listened to farmers tell stories. He quickly saw that there was poetry in their lively way of talking. He learned to listen for the beauty in ordinary speech, what he called "the sound of sense," which is the music of language in conversation. Frost's poems became conversational, using simple words but combining them in ways that made them extremely memorable.

Few other poets have captured the lives of ordinary people, their dreams and fears, their joy and grief, as succinctly as Robert Frost. His poetry remains a vivid testament to the wonders of nature, the pleasures and pains of farming, and the importance of poetic language as a way of framing experience and underscoring the work of thought and feeling in the creation of life itself.

The Pasture

I'm going out to clean the pasture spring;
I'll only stop to rake the leaves away
(And wait to watch the water clear, I may):
I sha'n't be gone long.—You come too.

I'm going out to fetch the little calf
That's standing by the mother. It's so young,
It totters when she licks it with her tongue.
I sha'n't be gone long.—You come too.

Totters — wobbles, wavers

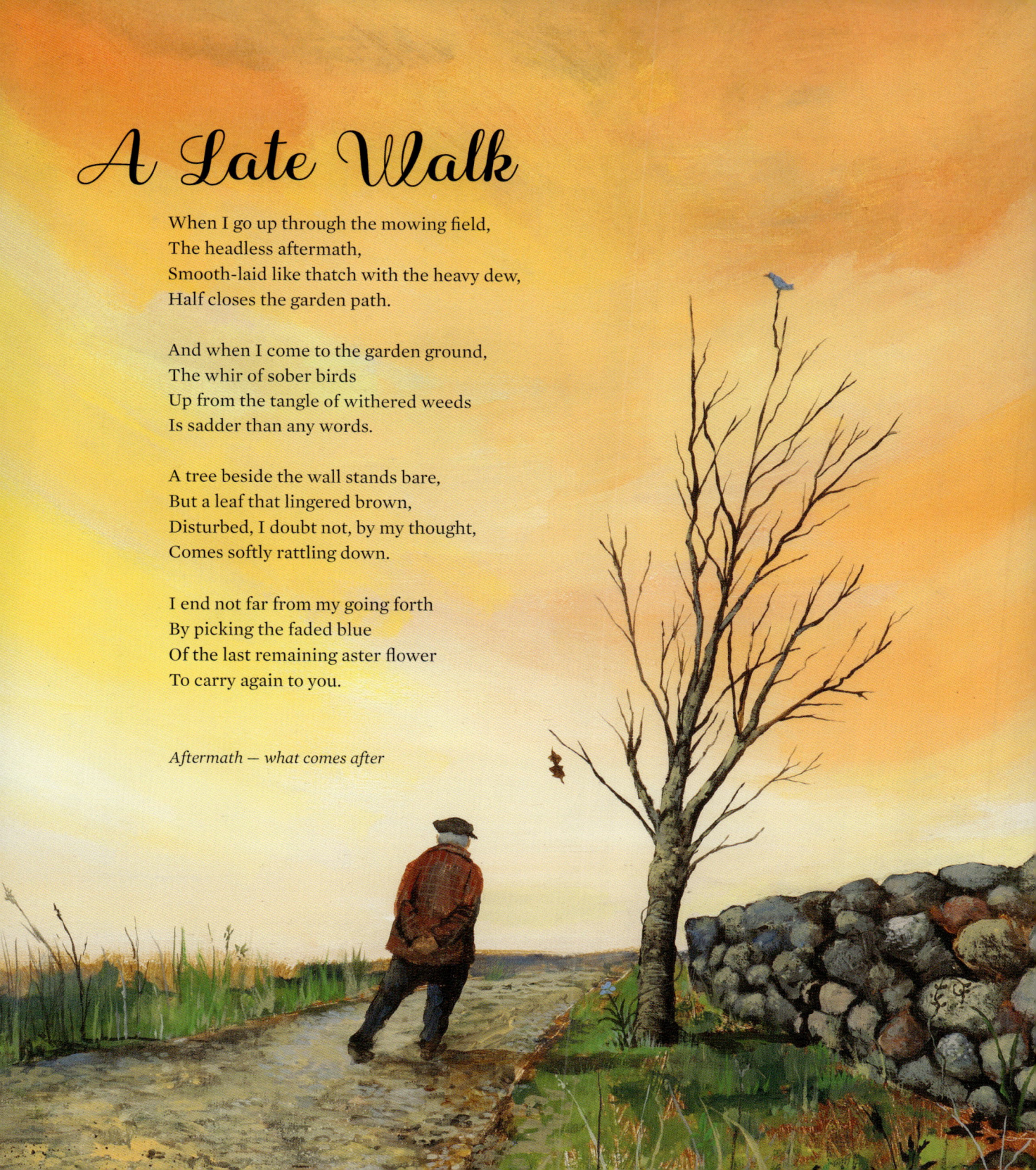

A Late Walk

When I go up through the mowing field,
The headless aftermath,
Smooth-laid like thatch with the heavy dew,
Half closes the garden path.

And when I come to the garden ground,
The whir of sober birds
Up from the tangle of withered weeds
Is sadder than any words.

A tree beside the wall stands bare,
But a leaf that lingered brown,
Disturbed, I doubt not, by my thought,
Comes softly rattling down.

I end not far from my going forth
By picking the faded blue
Of the last remaining aster flower
To carry again to you.

Aftermath — what comes after

Into My Own

One of my wishes is that those dark trees,
So old and firm they scarcely show the breeze,
Were not, as 'twere, the merest mask of gloom,
But stretched away unto the edge of doom.

I should not be withheld but that some day
Into their vastness I should steal away,
Fearless of ever finding open land,
Or highway where the slow wheel pours the sand.

I do not see why I should e'er turn back,
Or those should not set forth upon my track
To overtake me, who should miss me here
And long to know if still I held them dear.

They would not find me changed from him they knew—
Only more sure of all I thought was true.

'Twere — as it were
Steal away — sneak away
E'er — ever

11

Ghost House

I dwell in a lonely house I know
That vanished many a summer ago,
And left no trace but the cellar walls,
And a cellar in which the daylight falls,
And the purple-stemmed wild raspberries grow.

O'er ruined fences the grape-vines shield
The woods come back to the mowing field;
The orchard tree has grown one copse
Of new wood and old where the woodpecker chops;
The footpath down to the well is healed.

I dwell with a strangely aching heart
In that vanished abode there far apart
On that disused and forgotten road
That has no dust-bath now for the toad.
Night comes; the black bats tumble and dart;

The whippoorwill is coming to shout
And hush and cluck and flutter about:
I hear him begin far enough away
Full many a time to say his say
Before he arrives to say it out.

It is under the small, dim, summer star.
I know not who these mute folk are
Who share the unlit place with me—
Those stones out under the low-limbed tree
Doubtless bear names that the mosses mar.

They are tireless folk, but slow and sad,
Though two, close-keeping, are lass and lad,—
With none among them that ever sings,
And yet, in view of how many things,
As sweet companions as might be had.

Copse — orchard or field
Dart — skip around
Whippoorwill — a small bird that sings at night
Mar — blemish

My November Guest

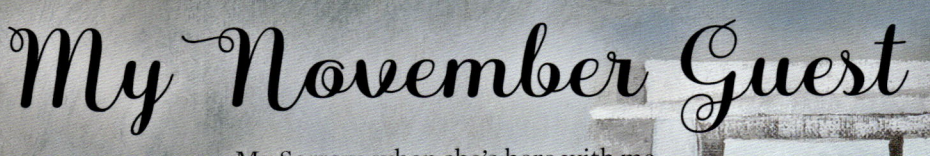

My Sorrow, when she's here with me,
Thinks these dark days of autumn rain
Are beautiful as days can be;
She loves the bare, the withered tree;
She walks the sodden pasture lane.

Her pleasure will not let me stay.
She talks and I am fain to list:
She's glad the birds are gone away,
She's glad her simple worsted gray
Is silver now with clinging mist.

The desolate, deserted trees,
The faded earth, the heavy sky,
The beauties she so truly sees,
She thinks I have no eye for these,
And vexes me for reason why.

Not yesterday I learned to know
The love of bare November days
Before the coming of the snow,
But it were vain to tell her so,
And they are better for her praise.

Sodden — wet
Fain — bound or determined to listen
Worsted — like a fabric
Vain — futile, hopeless

Stars

How countlessly they congregate
O'er our tumultuous snow,
Which flows in shapes as tall as trees
When wintry winds do blow!—

As if with keenness for our fate,
Our faltering few steps on
To white rest, and a place of rest
Invisible at dawn,—

And yet with neither love nor hate,
Those stars like some snow-white
Minerva's snow-white marble eyes
Without the gift of sight.

Congregate — gather
Tumultuous — bountiful or heavy
Keenness — interest, eagerness
Minerva —goddess of wisdom in ancient Rome

Storm Fear

When the wind works against us in the dark,
And pelts with snow
The lowest chamber window on the east,
And whispers with a sort of stifled bark,
The beast,
'Come out! Come out!'—
It costs no inward struggle not to go,
Ah, no!
I count our strength,
Two and a child,
Those of us not asleep subdued to mark
How the cold creeps as the fire dies at length,—
How drifts are piled,
Dooryard and road ungraded,
Till even the comforting barn grows far away
And my heart owns a doubt
Whether 'tis in us to arise with day
And save ourselves unaided.

Stifled —suppressed or muffled
Subdued — quieted
Mark — note
Ungraded — not smoothed

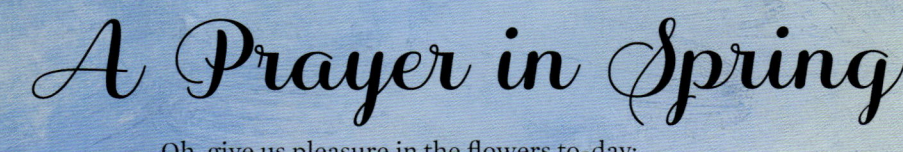

A Prayer in Spring

Oh, give us pleasure in the flowers to-day;
And give us not to think so far away
As the uncertain harvest; keep us here
All simply in the springing of the year.

Oh, give us pleasure in the orchard white,
Like nothing else by day, like ghosts by night;
And make us happy in the happy bees,
The swarm dilating round the perfect trees.

And make us happy in the darting bird
That suddenly above the bees is heard,
The meteor that thrusts in with needle bill,
And off a blossom in mid air stands still.

For this is love and nothing else is love,
The which it is reserved for God above
To sanctify to what far ends He will,
But which it only needs that we fulfil.

Dilating — expanding, growing
Meteor — like a shooting star
Sanctify — make holy

Flower-Gathering

I left you in the morning,
And in the morning glow,
You walked a way beside me
To make me sad to go.
Do you know me in the gloaming,
Gaunt and dusty grey with roaming?
Are you dumb because you know me not,
Or dumb because you know?

All for me? And not a question
For the faded flowers gay
That could take me from beside you
For the ages of a day?
They are yours, and be the measure
Of their worth for you to treasure,
The measure of the little while
That I've been long away.

Gloaming — dusk
Gaunt — lean or haggard
Dumb — silent
Gay — brightly colored

Mowing

There was never a sound beside the wood but one,
And that was my long scythe whispering to the ground.
What was it it whispered? I knew not well myself;
Perhaps it was something about the heat of the sun,
Something, perhaps, about the lack of sound—
And that was why it whispered and did not speak.
It was no dream of the gift of idle hours,
Or easy gold at the hand of fay or elf:
Anything more than the truth would have seemed too weak
To the earnest love that laid the swale in rows,
Not without feeble-pointed spikes of flowers
(Pale orchises), and scared a bright green snake.
The fact is the sweetest dream that labor knows.
My long scythe whispered and left the hay to make.

Scythe — tool for cutting grass
Fay — imaginary fairy creature
Swale — low field on a farm

An Old Man's Winter Night

All out of doors looked darkly in at him
Through the thin frost, almost in separate stars,
That gathers on the pane in empty rooms.
What kept his eyes from giving back the gaze
Was the lamp tilted near them in his hand.
What kept him from remembering what it was
That brought him to that creaking room was age.
He stood with barrels round him—at a loss.
And having scared the cellar under him
In clomping there, he scared it once again
In clomping off;—and scared the outer night,
Which has its sounds, familiar, like the roar
Of trees and crack of branches, common things,
But nothing so like beating on a box.
A light he was to no one but himself
Where now he sat, concerned with he knew what,
A quiet light, and then not even that.
He consigned to the moon, such as she was,
So late-arising, to the broken moon
As better than the sun in any case
For such a charge, his snow upon the roof,
His icicles along the wall to keep;
And slept. The log that shifted with a jolt
Once in the stove, disturbed him and he shifted,
And eased his heavy breathing, but still slept.
One aged man—one man—can't fill a house,
A farm, a countryside, or if he can,
It's thus he does it of a winter night.

Clomping — stomping
Consigned — gave away rights
Charge — argument, claim

Going for Water

The well was dry beside the door,
And so we went with pail and can
Across the fields behind the house
To seek the brook if still it ran;

Not loth to have excuse to go,
Because the autumn eve was fair
(Though chill), because the fields were ours,
And by the brook our woods were there.

We ran as if to meet the moon
That slowly dawned behind the trees,
The barren boughs without the leaves,
Without the birds, without the breeze.

But once within the wood, we paused
Like gnomes that hid us from the moon,
Ready to run to hiding new
With laughter when she found us soon.

Each laid on other a staying hand
To listen ere we dared to look,
And in the hush we joined to make
We heard, we knew we heard the brook.

A note as from a single place,
A slender tinkling fall that made
Now drops that floated on the pool
Like pearls, and now a silver blade.

Ran — bubbled away
Loth — sorry
Barren — bare, empty
Staying — steadying
Ere — before

23

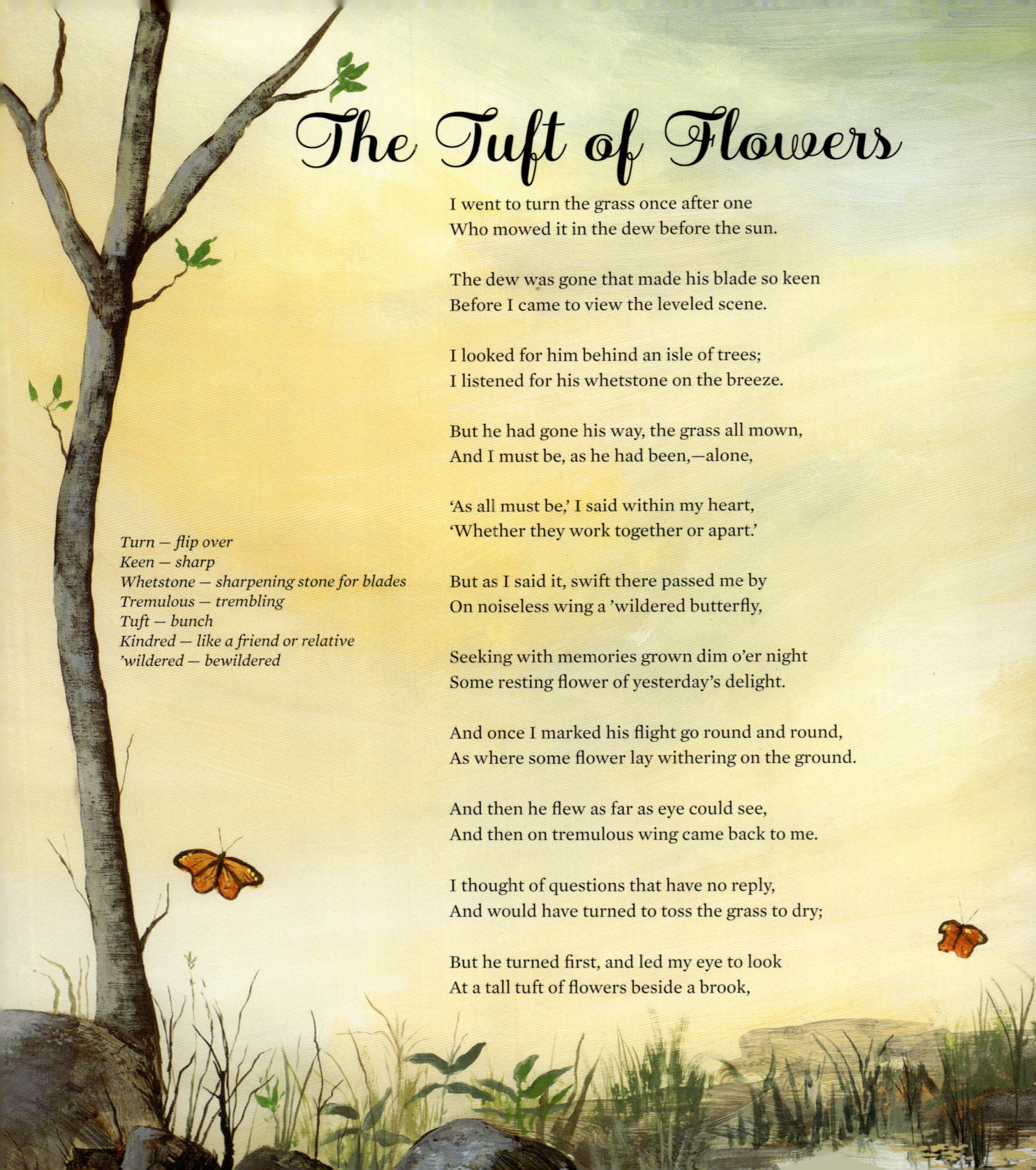

The Tuft of Flowers

I went to turn the grass once after one
Who mowed it in the dew before the sun.

The dew was gone that made his blade so keen
Before I came to view the leveled scene.

I looked for him behind an isle of trees;
I listened for his whetstone on the breeze.

But he had gone his way, the grass all mown,
And I must be, as he had been,—alone,

'As all must be,' I said within my heart,
'Whether they work together or apart.'

But as I said it, swift there passed me by
On noiseless wing a 'wildered butterfly,

Seeking with memories grown dim o'er night
Some resting flower of yesterday's delight.

And once I marked his flight go round and round,
As where some flower lay withering on the ground.

And then he flew as far as eye could see,
And then on tremulous wing came back to me.

I thought of questions that have no reply,
And would have turned to toss the grass to dry;

But he turned first, and led my eye to look
At a tall tuft of flowers beside a brook,

Turn — flip over
Keen — sharp
Whetstone — sharpening stone for blades
Tremulous — trembling
Tuft — bunch
Kindred — like a friend or relative
'wildered — bewildered

A leaping tongue of bloom the scythe had spared
Beside a reedy brook the scythe had bared.

I left my place to know them by their name,
Finding them butterfly weed when I came.

The mower in the dew had loved them thus,
By leaving them to flourish, not for us,

Nor yet to draw one thought of ours to him.
But from sheer morning gladness at the brim.

The butterfly and I had lit upon,
Nevertheless, a message from the dawn,

That made me hear the wakening birds around,
And hear his long scythe whispering to the ground,

And feel a spirit kindred to my own;
So that henceforth I worked no more alone;

But glad with him, I worked as with his aid,
And weary, sought at noon with him the shade;

And dreaming, as it were, held brotherly speech
With one whose thought I had not hoped to reach.

'Men work together,' I told him from the heart,
'Whether they work together or apart.'

October

O hushed October morning mild,
Thy leaves have ripened to the fall;
To-morrow's wind, if it be wild,
Should waste them all.
The crows above the forest call;
To-morrow they may form and go.
O hushed October morning mild,
Begin the hours of this day slow,
Make the day seem to us less brief.
Hearts not averse to being beguiled,
Beguile us in the way you know;
Release one leaf at break of day;
At noon release another leaf;
One from our trees, one far away;
Retard the sun with gentle mist;
Enchant the land with amethyst.
Slow, slow!
For the grapes' sake, if they were all,
Whose leaves already are burnt with frost,
Whose clustered fruit must else be lost—
For the grapes' sake along the wall.

26

Waste — blow away
Averse — against
Beguile — fascinate, draw toward
Retard — hold back

Reluctance

Out through the fields and the woods
And over the walls I have wended;
I have climbed the hills of view
And looked at the world, and descended;
I have come by the highway home,
And lo, it is ended.

The leaves are all dead on the ground,
Save those that the oak is keeping
To ravel them one by one
And let them go scraping and creeping
Out over the crusted snow,
When others are sleeping.

And the dead leaves lie huddled and still,
No longer blown hither and thither;
The last lone aster is gone;
The flowers of the witch-hazel wither;
The heart is still aching to seek,
But the feet question 'Whither?'

Ah, when to the heart of man
Was it ever less than a treason
To go with the drift of things,
To yield with a grace to reason,
And bow and accept the end
Of a love or a season?

Wended — weaved a way
Save — except
Ravel — bind together
Hither and thither — here and there

Mending Wall

Something there is that doesn't love a wall,
That sends the frozen-ground-swell under it,
And spills the upper boulders in the sun;
And makes gaps even two can pass abreast.
The work of hunters is another thing:
I have come after them and made repair
Where they have left not one stone on a stone,
But they would have the rabbit out of hiding,
To please the yelping dogs. The gaps I mean,
No one has seen them made or heard them made,
But at spring mending-time we find them there.
I let my neighbour know beyond the hill;
And on a day we meet to walk the line
And set the wall between us once again.
We keep the wall between us as we go.
To each the boulders that have fallen to each.
And some are loaves and some so nearly balls
We have to use a spell to make them balance:
"Stay where you are until our backs are turned!"
We wear our fingers rough with handling them.
Oh, just another kind of out-door game,
One on a side. It comes to little more:
There where it is we do not need the wall:

He is all pine and I am apple orchard.
My apple trees will never get across
And eat the cones under his pines, I tell him.
He only says, "Good fences make good neighbours."
Spring is the mischief in me, and I wonder
If I could put a notion in his head:
"*Why* do they make good neighbours? Isn't it
Where there are cows? But here there are no cows.
Before I built a wall I'd ask to know
What I was walling in or walling out,
And to whom I was like to give offence.
Something there is that doesn't love a wall,
That wants it down." I could say "Elves" to him,
But it's not elves exactly, and I'd rather
He said it for himself. I see him there
Bringing a stone grasped firmly by the top
In each hand, like an old-stone savage armed.
He moves in darkness as it seems to me,
Not of woods only and the shade of trees.
He will not go behind his father's saying,
And he likes having thought of it so well
He says again, "Good fences make good neighbours."

Abreast — near to each other
Notion — idea
Offence — insult

After Apple-Picking

My long two-pointed ladder's sticking through a tree
Toward heaven still,
And there's a barrel that I didn't fill
Beside it, and there may be two or three
Apples I didn't pick upon some bough.
But I am done with apple-picking now.
Essence of winter sleep is on the night,
The scent of apples: I am drowsing off.
I cannot rub the strangeness from my sight
I got from looking through a pane of glass
I skimmed this morning from the drinking trough
And held against the world of hoary grass.
It melted, and I let it fall and break.
But I was well
Upon my way to sleep before it fell,
And I could tell
What form my dreaming was about to take.
Magnified apples appear and disappear,
Stem end and blossom end,
And every fleck of russet showing clear.
My instep arch not only keeps the ache,
It keeps the pressure of a ladder-round.
I feel the ladder sway as the boughs bend.
And I keep hearing from the cellar bin
The rumbling sound
Of load on load of apples coming in.
For I have had too much
Of apple-picking: I am overtired
Of the great harvest I myself desired.

There were ten thousand thousand fruit to touch,
Cherish in hand, lift down, and not let fall.
For all
That struck the earth,
No matter if not bruised or spiked with stubble,
Went surely to the cider-apple heap
As of no worth.
One can see what will trouble
This sleep of mine, whatever sleep it is.
Were he not gone,
The woodchuck could say whether it's like his
Long sleep, as I describe its coming on,
Or just some human sleep.

Bough — branch
Trough — feed box for animals
Hoary — gray
Fleck of russet — speck of red
Stubble — bits of grass

31

The Wood-Pile

Out walking in the frozen swamp one grey day
I paused and said, "I will turn back from here.
No, I will go on farther—and we shall see."
The hard snow held me, save where now and then
One foot went down. The view was all in lines
Straight up and down of tall slim trees
Too much alike to mark or name a place by
So as to say for certain I was here
Or somewhere else: I was just far from home.
A small bird flew before me. He was careful
To put a tree between us when he lighted,
And say no word to tell me who he was
Who was so foolish as to think what *he* thought.
He thought that I was after him for a feather—
The white one in his tail; like one who takes
Everything said as personal to himself.
One flight out sideways would have undeceived him.
And then there was a pile of wood for which
I forgot him and let his little fear
Carry him off the way I might have gone,
Without so much as wishing him good-night.
He went behind it to make his last stand.
It was a cord of maple, cut and split
And piled—and measured, four by four by eight.
And not another like it could I see.
No runner tracks in this year's snow looped near it.
And it was older sure than this year's cutting,
Or even last year's or the year's before.
The wood was grey and the bark warping off it
And the pile somewhat sunken. Clematis
Had wound strings round and round it like a bundle.

What held it though on one side was a tree
Still growing, and on one a stake and prop,
These latter about to fall. I thought that only
Someone who lived in turning to fresh tasks
Could so forget his handiwork on which
He spent himself, the labour of his axe,
And leave it there far from a useful fireplace
To warm the frozen swamp as best it could
With the slow smokeless burning of decay.

Lighted — landed
Undeceived — made him aware
Cord — pile
Warping — peeling
Clematis — a plant

The Road Not Taken

Two roads diverged in a yellow wood,
And sorry I could not travel both
And be one traveler, long I stood
And looked down one as far as I could
To where it bent in the undergrowth;

Then took the other, as just as fair,
And having perhaps the better claim,
Because it was grassy and wanted wear;
Though as for that the passing there
Had worn them really about the same,

Claim — right or stake
Wear — had not been walked on
Way — path

And both that morning equally lay
In leaves no step had trodden black.
Oh, I kept the first for another day!
Yet knowing how way leads on to way,
I doubted if I should ever come back.

I shall be telling this with a sigh
Somewhere ages and ages hence:
Two roads diverged in a wood, and I—
I took the one less traveled by,
And that has made all the difference.

Hyla Brook

By June our brook's run out of song and speed.
Sought for much after that, it will be found
Either to have gone groping underground
(And taken with it all the Hyla breed
That shouted in the mist a month ago,
Like ghost of sleigh-bells in a ghost of snow)—
Or flourished and come up in jewel-weed,
Weak foliage that is blown upon and bent
Even against the way its waters went.
Its bed is left a faded paper sheet
Of dead leaves stuck together by the heat—
A brook to none but who remember long.
This as it will be seen is other far
Than with brooks taken otherwhere in song.
We love the things we love for what they are.

Groping — sneaking
Hyla breed — a kind of flower

The Oven Bird

There is a singer everyone has heard,
Loud, a mid-summer and a mid-wood bird,
Who makes the solid tree trunks sound again.
He says that leaves are old and that for flowers
Mid-summer is to spring as one to ten.
He says the early petal-fall is past
When pear and cherry bloom went down in showers
On sunny days a moment overcast;
And comes that other fall we name the fall.
He says the highway dust is over all.
The bird would cease and be as other birds
But that he knows in singing not to sing.
The question that he frames in all but words
Is what to make of a diminished thing.

Diminished — less than perfect

Birches

When I see birches bend to left and right
Across the lines of straighter darker trees,
I like to think some boy's been swinging them.
But swinging doesn't bend them down to stay.
Ice-storms do that. Often you must have seen them
Loaded with ice a sunny winter morning
After a rain. They click upon themselves
As the breeze rises, and turn many-colored
As the stir cracks and crazes their enamel.
Soon the sun's warmth makes them shed crystal shells
Shattering and avalanching on the snow-crust—
Such heaps of broken glass to sweep away
You'd think the inner dome of heaven had fallen.
They are dragged to the withered bracken by the load,
And they seem not to break; though once they are bowed
So low for long, they never right themselves:
You may see their trunks arching in the woods
Years afterwards, trailing their leaves on the ground
Like girls on hands and knees that throw their hair
Before them over their heads to dry in the sun.
But I was going to say when Truth broke in
With all her matter-of-fact about the ice-storm
(Now am I free to be poetical?)
I should prefer to have some boy bend them
As he went out and in to fetch the cows—
Some boy too far from town to learn baseball,
Whose only play was what he found himself,
Summer or winter, and could play alone.
One by one he subdued his father's trees
By riding them down over and over again
Until he took the stiffness out of them,
And not one but hung limp, not one was left
For him to conquer. He learned all there was
To learn about not launching out too soon

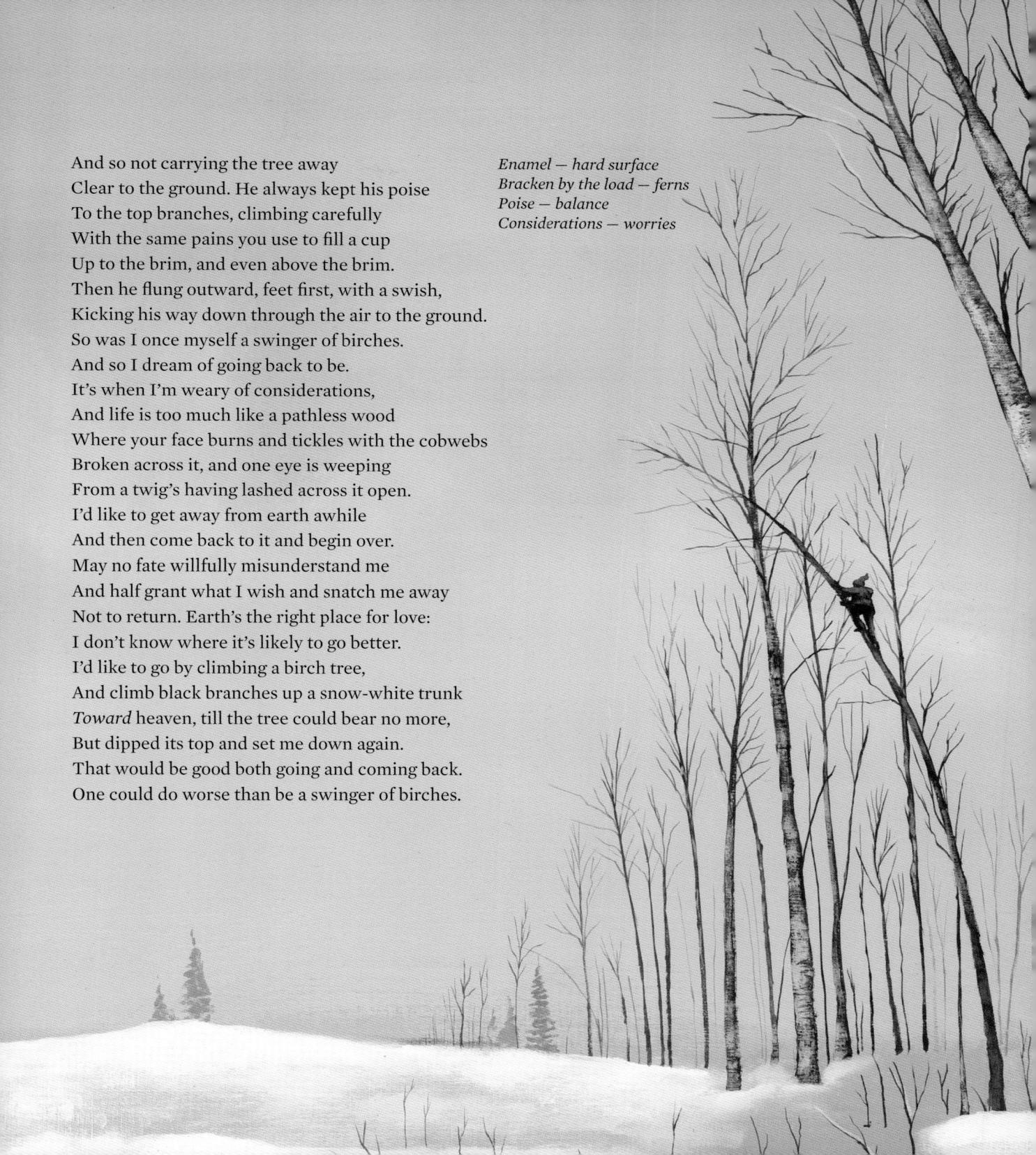

And so not carrying the tree away
Clear to the ground. He always kept his poise
To the top branches, climbing carefully
With the same pains you use to fill a cup
Up to the brim, and even above the brim.
Then he flung outward, feet first, with a swish,
Kicking his way down through the air to the ground.
So was I once myself a swinger of birches.
And so I dream of going back to be.
It's when I'm weary of considerations,
And life is too much like a pathless wood
Where your face burns and tickles with the cobwebs
Broken across it, and one eye is weeping
From a twig's having lashed across it open.
I'd like to get away from earth awhile
And then come back to it and begin over.
May no fate willfully misunderstand me
And half grant what I wish and snatch me away
Not to return. Earth's the right place for love:
I don't know where it's likely to go better.
I'd like to go by climbing a birch tree,
And climb black branches up a snow-white trunk
Toward heaven, till the tree could bear no more,
But dipped its top and set me down again.
That would be good both going and coming back.
One could do worse than be a swinger of birches.

Enamel — hard surface
Bracken by the load — ferns
Poise — balance
Considerations — worries

Putting in the Seed

You come to fetch me from my work to-night
When supper's on the table, and we'll see
If I can leave off burying the white
Soft petals fallen from the apple tree.

(Soft petals, yes, but not so barren quite,
Mingled with these, smooth bean and wrinkled pea;)
And go along with you ere you lose sight
Of what you came for and become like me,

Slave to a springtime passion for the earth.
How Love burns through the Putting in the Seed
On through the watching for that early birth
When, just as the soil tarnishes with weed,

The sturdy seedling with arched body comes
Shouldering its way and shedding the earth crumbs.

Barren — wasted
Tarnishes — rusts or is ruined by
crumbs [bits of soil]

The Cow in Apple Time

Something inspires the only cow of late
To make no more of a wall than an open gate,
And think no more of wall-builders than fools.
Her face is flecked with pomace and she drools
A cider syrup. Having tasted fruit,
She scorns a pasture withering to the root.
She runs from tree to tree where lie and sweeten
The windfalls spiked with stubble and worm-eaten.
She leaves them bitten when she has to fly.
She bellows on a knoll against the sky.
Her udder shrivels and the milk goes dry.

Pomace — pulpy substance
Bellows — shouts

41

"Out, Out—"

The buzz-saw snarled and rattled in the yard
And made dust and dropped stove-length sticks of wood,
Sweet-scented stuff when the breeze drew across it.
And from there those that lifted eyes could count
Five mountain ranges one behind the other
Under the sunset far into Vermont.
And the saw snarled and rattled, snarled and rattled,
As it ran light, or had to bear a load.
And nothing happened: day was all but done.
Call it a day, I wish they might have said
To please the boy by giving him the half hour
That a boy counts so much when saved from work.
His sister stood beside them in her apron
To tell them "Supper." At the word, the saw,
As if to prove saws knew what supper meant,
Leaped out at the boy's hand, or seemed to leap—
He must have given the hand. However it was,
Neither refused the meeting. But the hand!

The boy's first outcry was a rueful laugh,
As he swung toward them holding up the hand
Half in appeal, but half as if to keep
The life from spilling. Then the boy saw all—
Since he was old enough to know, big boy
Doing a man's work, though a child at heart—
He saw all spoiled. "Don't let him cut my hand off—
The doctor, when he comes. Don't let him, sister!"
So. But the hand was gone already.
The doctor put him in the dark of ether.
He lay and puffed his lips out with his breath.
And then—the watcher at his pulse took fright.
No one believed. They listened at his heart.
Little—less—nothing!—and that ended it.
No more to build on there. And they, since they
Were not the one dead, turned to their affairs.

Drew — moved
Counts — values
Rueful — sad
Appeal — hope
Ether — a gas that knocks you out
Affairs — business

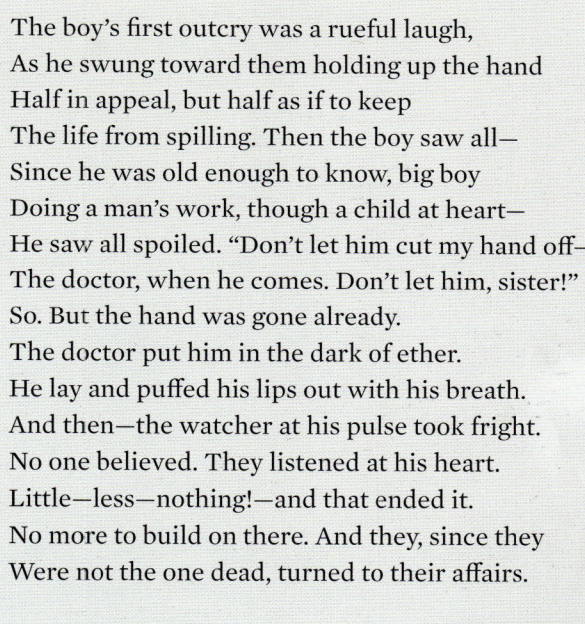

To the Thawing Wind

Come with rain, O loud Southwester!
Bring the singer, bring the nester;
Give the buried flower a dream;
Make the settled snow-bank steam;
Find the brown beneath the white;
But whate'er you do to-night,
Bathe my window, make it flow,
Melt it as the ices go;

Melt the glass and leave the sticks
Like a hermit's crucifix;
Burst into my narrow stall;
Swing the picture on the wall;
Run the rattling pages o'er;
Scatter poems on the floor;
Turn the poet out of door.

Hermit — a solitary man
Crucifix — a cross
Stall — room

Snow Dust

The way a crow
Shook down on me
The dust of snow
From a hemlock tree

Has given my heart
A change of mood
And saved some part
Of a day I had rued.

Rued — regretted

What Robert Was Thinking

The Pasture: This poem is an invitation to Frost's world of green fields, cows, and simple pleasure.

A Late Walk: After a day's work, with the fields mown, the speaker walks into the pasture and thinks of a loved one, for whom he picks a flower.

Into My Own: The poet asserts his own awareness of himself in the world, a place where he has a strong sense of his own values and disposition.

Ghost House: In this poem, a house becomes a representative of the poet's soul, a dwelling he recalls with nostalgia.

My November Guest: The poet thinks of his sorrow, which seems a constant visitor in November, as he looks forward to winter with some apprehension.

Stars: Stars have always fascinated poets, and Frost is no exception. This poem is a lovely meditation on the vivid lights that fill the sky on a winter's night.

Storm Fear: This haunting poem is about a small family that experiences the pounding wind of a storm outside their little house. They feel tremendously afraid. At the same time, there is strength in their family of three, and they can huddle together to overcome this fear.

A Prayer in Spring: The poem is a beautiful prayer for a season that brings all sorts of bounty and promise, including white blossoms on fruit trees.

Flower-Gathering: This haunting poem is addressed to a loved one. It poses many questions, all of them concerning the bouquet of flowers that the speaker has picked.

Mowing: This remains one of Frost's best early poems. It's about mowing a field to make hay, but it's also about writing. The poet uses his pen to find things out about the world. It's how he pursued the difficult work of knowing.

An Old Man's Winter Night: This is an eerie poem about an old man who seems at the end of his life. He can't "keep" anything anymore. Not a house, not a countryside, not himself. It's a beautiful poem, too, with the stars looking in on the old man.

Going for Water: As with many Frost poems, this is about a simple job. Going for water represents the human need for sustenance, for quenching our thirst. It is both a physical and emotional need.

The Tuft of Flowers: The speaker notices that a mower who has gone before him (and departed) has left a tuft of flowers out of sheer "morning gladness" at its beauty. The poet finds in this mysterious mower a kindred spirit and suggests that there is a common bond that unites people even when they work separately.

October: The seasons mean a great deal to this poet, who reads them closely, looking for signs that are emotional, spiritual, and physical.

Reluctance: Human beings are reluctant to let go of anything—love or a season that they love. This poem notices and celebrates that slight hesitation that everyone feels at times when the season has passed and one must let go of something very dear.

Mending Wall: The speaker summons a neighbor to walk along and repair a dry stone wall, putting back stones that have tumbled through winter. The dialogue takes place mainly in the speaker's head, and it brings out the idea of two worlds. Is the wall a good thing or a bad thing? The speaker is against walls. But he can't resist the old saying: "Good fences make good neighbors," which he puts in the mouth of the neighbor, who represents an "old-stone savage."

After Apple-Picking: Apple picking is an important part of the farming world; however, the speaker in this poem is talking about more than apples. The apples are poems to be picked and preserved, let to fall to the ground and rot, or to be taken away to be pressed into cider. This is a poem about the end of a day, weariness itself, and even the end of a life.

The Wood-Pile: In many poems by Frost, a solitary man goes into the woods and measures himself against the natural world. Here he goes into a swamp and discovers a mysterious cord of wood. Who would take such trouble, cutting and stacking so much wood in a place where it seems quite useless? Is this somewhat like writing poems, stacking the lines, which are measured out carefully and left, perhaps, for nobody to read?

The Road Not Taken: This is Frost's most famous poem, and it's about the classic "fork in the road." Notice that the two paths are "really about the same" in how worn they may be. The poem is a tricky one that needs to be read carefully. In the last two lines, the speaker declares that by taking one road and not another this made "all the difference." How can that be when "both that morning equally lay?"

Hyla Brook: Many of Frost's poems are about inspiration, and the brook in this poem is about just that: inspiration that goes underground at times, hidden from view. Just as the brook will reemerge in flowers—jewelweeds—the poet's hidden inspiration will emerge as poetry.

The Oven Bird: An ovenbird is common in the woods of New England, but it has a rather flat chirping sound. It knows "in singing not to sing." The bird is like the poet who Frost imagines—who thinks about a world where nothing is quite like it used to be. Frost seems to identify with this bird and see his work as similar to that of the poet in the poem.

Birches: Boys in New England used to like to climb birch trees to find their tipping point, where they bend to the earth. The poet takes this a step further, building a whole story about the best place for love. Is it heaven or earth? The answer is clear: "Earth's the best place for love."

Putting in the Seed: In another of Frost's poems about work, the work of planting is important. The farmer puts the flower petals into the earth as fertilizer, but in this poem, the writer wonders about where the reward for this work lies. Is it in the act of putting the seed in the ground or watching the sprouts that will come later?

The Cow in Apple Time: This is a funny poem about a cow that breaks through a wall into an apple orchard and gorges on fruit that ferment in her stomach and upset her system so that she can't produce milk. The poem suggests that animals, including humans, never seem quite satisfied with what they have, and how yearning can produce ill effects.

"Out, Out —": This tragedy, which is about the accidental death of a boy on a farm at the turn of the twentieth century, actually happened in Frost's neighborhood. He was very moved by the story and recreates it with tremendous force. The poem is about—among many things—how poor farmers deal with the loss of a hand (which has multiple meanings). It's mainly a poem about death and how one deals with unexpected horrors like this.

To the Thawing Wind: The wind seems like a chaotic force in this poem, affecting the world, the house, the poet, and his poems. It scatters everything, and the poet celebrates this wild energy.

Snow Dust: A little instance of movement in nature can shake a person into awareness. In this poem, snow is being shaken down to the ground and lands on the speaker.

index

The Poetry Collection

Emily Dickinson

THE POETRY COLLECTION

Emily Dickinson

ILLUSTRATED BY
CHRISTINE DAVENIER

EDITED BY SUSAN SNIVELY, PHD

MoonDance

Publisher's Note

Many years ago, my grandmother read poetry to me at a very young age, even Shakespeare. She felt, as I now can appreciate, that the emotion and mood of poetry, even when it is almost too hard to understand, is so essential to understanding the world around us. I'm hoping that this series, with its selection of a very diverse group of poets, and with art by some of the world's best illustrators, will bring that all to life for a new generation. –Charles Nurnberg

Brimming with creative inspiration, how-to projects, and useful information to enrich your everyday life, Quarto Knows is a favorite destination for those pursuing their interests and passions. Visit our site and dig deeper with our books into your area of interest: Quarto Creates, Quarto Cooks, Quarto Homes, Quarto Lives, Quarto Drives, Quarto Explores, Quarto Gifts, or Quarto Kids.

© 2018 Quarto Publishing Group USA Inc.
Original text © 2016 Susan Snively
Illustrations © 2016 Christine Davenier

First Published in 2016 by Published by MoonDance Press, an imprint of The Quarto Group.
26391 Crown Valley Parkway, Suite 220, Mission Viejo, CA 92691, USA.
T (949) 380-7510 F (949) 380-7575 www.QuartoKnows.com

Walter Foster Publishing titles are also available at discount for retail, wholesale, promotional, and bulk purchase. For details, contact the Special Sales Manager by email at specialsales@quarto.com or by mail at The Quarto Group, Attn: Special Sales Manager, 100 Cummings Center, Suite 265D, Beverly, MA 01915, USA.

ISBN: 978-1-63322-117-8

Digital edition published in 2016
eISBN: 978-1-63322-309-7

Cover design and layout by Melissa Gerber

Printed in Guangdong, China
10 9 8 7 6 5 4 3 2 1
November 2019
19090228

Contents

Introduction

EMILY DICKINSON WAS BORN ON DECEMBER 10, 1830, AND DIED ON MAY 15, 1886.

She lived in Amherst, Massachusetts, all her life, occupying a large brick house on Main Street near a huge meadow, the railroad station, and a hat factory. Two blocks away was Amherst College, which her grandfather Samuel Fowler Dickinson had helped to found in 1821. Emily's father, Edward, was a lawyer, treasurer of Amherst College, a member of the General Court of Massachusetts, and, briefly, a US congressman. He married Emily Norcross of Monson, Massachusetts, in May 1828. A quiet, sweet-natured woman, Emily Norcross was well educated and especially talented at gardening and baking. She and Edward had three children: Austin, born in 1829; Emily; and Lavinia, born in 1833. The smart, lively children shared a love of reading, music, nature, and each other's company.

Edward Dickinson helped to bring the railroad to the small town in 1853. Emily frequently heard the train's "horrid, hooting stanza," the whistles from the hat factory, and even the sounds of tumbling acrobats and caged animals moving along Main Street in the middle of the night when the circus came to town. The large windows of The Homestead showed Emily the dramas of the changing seasons and of life in "a country town."

The poet's life was both quiet and busy. She visited Washington, DC, and also journeyed to Philadelphia, Hartford, Worcester, Springfield, Boston, and Cambridge. Yet Emily Dickinson felt most comfortable at home. "Home is a holy thing," she remarked. She baked bread for the household, worked in the huge garden, wrote possibly ten thousand letters—think of what she might have done with e-mail!—and created poems that were unlike anybody else's poems: full of word-play, startling images, puzzles, and surprises.

In her mid-thirties, Emily developed a severe eye problem and was treated in Boston, where she stayed with her cousins Louisa and Frances Norcross. After "months of Siberia," she eventually improved. In 1874, her father, Edward, died unexpectedly of a stroke, and the following year, Emily's mother suffered a stroke that left her dependent on her daughters and their servant and friend Maggie Maher. Emily gradually withdrew from social activity, although she enjoyed visits from her good friends and baked gingerbread for the neighborhood children. The care of her mother, her devotion to writing poetry, and the pleasures of gardening took much of Emily's time.

Emily Dickinson's poems are populated by the birds, insects, frogs, snakes, and other creatures she observed on her property. Their activities, lives, and deaths seem like those of her relations. Her lifelong interest in science, especially botany and astronomy, enriched her language with beauty and wonder.

Emily died at age fifty-five in 1886, of hypertension, leaving behind a treasure trove of nearly 1,800 poems. In November 1890, her first volume, edited by Thomas Wentworth Higginson and Mabel Loomis Todd, was published, and went into eleven printings in one year. Now her readers can view her poems online (http://www.edickinson.org/), decipher her quirky handwriting, study the words she played with, and, as her sister, Lavinia, predicted, behold the poet's "genius."

Summer

It's all I have to bring today

It's all I have to bring today,
  This, and my heart beside,
This, and my heart, and all the fields,
  And all the meadows wide.
Be sure you count, should I forget,
  Some one the sum could tell,
This, and my heart, and all the bees
  Which in the clover dwell.

In the name of the Bee

In the name of the Bee —
And of the Butterfly —
And of the Breeze — Amen!

9

I'm nobody! Who are you?

I'm nobody! Who are you?
Are you nobody, too?
Then there's a pair of us — don't tell!
They'd banish us, you know.

How dreary to be somebody!
How public, like a frog
To tell your name the livelong day
To an admiring bog!

livelong — whole
bog — muddy swamp

A bird came down the walk

A bird came down the walk
He did not know I saw;
He bit an angleworm in halves
And ate the fellow, raw.

And then he drank a dew
From a convenient grass,
And then hopped sidewise to the wall
To let a beetle pass.

He glanced with rapid eyes
That hurried all abroad,
They looked like frightened beads, I thought;
He stirred his velvet head

Like one in danger; cautious,
I offered him a crumb,
And he unrolled his feathers
And rowed him softer home

Than oars divide the ocean,
Too silver for a seam,
Or butterflies, off banks of noon,
Leap, plashless, as they swim.

seam — ripple, furrow
plashless — smoothly, without splashing

11

They dropped like Flakes

They dropped like Flakes
They dropped like stars
Like Petals from a Rose
When suddenly across the June
A Wind with fingers goes

They perished in the seamless Grass
No eye could find the place
But God can summon every face
On his Repealless List.

flakes — snowflakes
stars — shooting stars, meteors
perished — died
seamless — without furrows
repealless — endless, from which
 nothing is erased

"Answer, July!"

"Answer, July! —
Where is the Bee —
Where is the Blush —
Where is the Hay?"

"Ah," said July,
"Where is the Seed —
Where is the Bud —
Where is the May? —
  Answer Thee me!"

"Nay," said the May,
"Show me the Snow —
Show me the Bells —
Show me the Jay!"

Quibbled the Jay,
"Where be the Maize —
Where be the Haze —
Where be the Burr?
  "Here!" — said the Year.

quibbled — answered
maize — corn
burr — seedpod

13

A narrow fellow in the grass

A narrow fellow in the grass
Occasionally rides;
You may have met him, — did you not?
His notice sudden is.

The grass divides as with a comb,
A spotted shaft is seen;
And then it closes at your feet
And opens further on.

He likes a boggy acre,
A floor too cool for corn.
Yet when a child, and barefoot,
I more than once, at morn,

Have passed, I thought, a whip-lash
Unbraiding in the sun, —
When, stooping to secure it,
It wrinkled, and was gone.

Several of nature's people
I know, and they know me;
I feel for them a transport
Of cordiality;

But never met this fellow,
Attended or alone,
Without a tighter breathing,
And zero at the bone.

shaft — dark, flash, snake
cordiality — friendly feeling
zero — freezing in the blood

Exhilaration is the breeze

Exhilaration is the breeze
That lifts us from the ground
And leaves us in another place
Whose statement is not found —
Returns us not, but after time
We soberly descend,
A little newer for the term
Upon enchanted ground.

exhilaration — joy, imagination
statement — definite meaning

To make a prairie it takes a clover and one bee

To make a prairie it takes a clover and one bee,
One clover, and a bee,
And revery.
The revery alone will do
If bees are few.

prairie — meadow
revery — daydream

A soft sea washed around the house

A soft sea washed around the house,
A sea of summer air,
And rose and fell the magic planks
That sailed without a care.

For captain was the butterfly,
For helmsman was the bee,
And an entire universe
For the delighted crew.

helmsman — one who steers a ship

From all the jails the boys and girls

From all the jails the boys and girls
  Ecstatically leap, —
Beloved, only afternoon
  That prison doesn't keep.

They storm the earth and stun the air,
  A mob of solid bliss.
Alas! that frowns could lie in wait
  For such a foe as this!

ecstatically — with wild joy

Autumn

The gentian weaves her fringes

The gentian weaves her fringes,
The maple's loom is red.
My departing blossoms
Obviate parade.

*gentian — purple wildflower
with white-fringed petals*
obviate — prevent

Faith is a fine invention

Faith is a fine invention
For gentlemen who see
But microscopes are prudent
In an emergency!

prudent — cautious and practical

Blazing in gold and quenching in purple

Blazing in gold and quenching in purple,
Leaping like leopards to the sky,
Then at the feet of the old horizon
Laying her spotted face, to die;

Stooping as low as the otter's window,
Touching the roof and tinting the barn,
Kissing her bonnet to the meadow, —
And the juggler of day is gone!

I never saw a moor

I never saw a moor.
I never saw the sea;
Yet know I how the heather looks,
And what a wave must be.

I never spoke with God,
Nor visited in heaven;
Yet certain am I of the spot
As if the chart were given.

moor — *bog or marsh*
heather — *purplish plant that grows on moors*
chart — *map*

He fumbles at your spirit

He fumbles at your spirit
  As players at the keys
Before they drop full music on
  He stuns you by degrees,

Prepares your brittle substance
  For the ethereal Blow
By fainter hammers, further heard,
  Then nearer, then so slow

Your breath has time to straighten
  Your brain to bubble cool, —
Deals one imperial thunderbolt
  That scalps your naked soul.

before they drop full music on — before they start playing
brittle — easily broken
ethereal — out of this world, mysterious
imperial — supreme, mighty

23

Because I could not stop for Death

Because I could not stop for Death,
He kindly stopped for me;
The carriage held but just ourselves
And Immortality.

We slowly drove, he knew no haste
And I had put away
My labor, and my leisure too,
For his civility.

We passed the school where children played,
Their lessons scarcely done;
We passed the fields of gazing grain,
We passed the setting sun.

We paused before a house that seemed
A swelling of the ground —
The roof was scarcely visible —
The cornice but a mound.

Since then 'tis centuries; but each
Feels shorter than the day
I first surmised the horses' heads
Were toward eternity.

leisure — play, relaxation
civility — courtesy, politeness
cornice — roof corner

25

The cricket sang

The cricket sang
And set the sun
And workmen finished one by one
Their seam the day upon.

The low grass loaded with the dew,
The twilight stood, as strangers do,
With hat in hand, polite and new
To stay as if, or go.

A vastness, as a neighbor, came,
A wisdom without face, or name,
A peace, as hemispheres at home,
And so the night became.

Winter

Safe in their alabaster chambers

Safe in their alabaster chambers,
Untouched by morning and untouched by noon,
Lie the meek members of the resurrection,
Rafter of satin and roof of stone.

Grand go the years in the crescent above them;
Worlds scoop their arcs, and firmaments row,
Diadems drop and Doges surrender,
Soundless as dots on a disc of snow.

alabaster — a pure white stone
resurrection — the revival of the dead
scoop — take out with a sweeping motion
firmaments — the sky or heavens
diadems — crowns
doges — rulers of Venice

27

It sifts from leaden sieves

It sifts from leaden sieves,
It powders all the wood,
It fills with alabaster wool
The wrinkles of the road.

It makes an even face
Of mountain and of plain, —
Unbroken forehead from the east
Unto the east again.

It reaches to the fence,
It wraps it, rail by rail,
Till it is lost in fleeces.
It flings a crystal veil

On stump and stack and stem, —
The summer's empty room,
Acres of seams where harvests were,
Recordless, but for them.

It ruffles wrists of posts,
As ankles of a queen, —
Then stills its artisans like ghosts,
Denying they have been.

leaden — gray and cold-looking
sieves — strainers

This is my letter to the world

This is my letter to the world,
  That never wrote to me, —
The simple news that Nature told,
  With tender majesty.

Her message is committed
  To hands I cannot see;
For love of her, sweet countrymen,
  Judge tenderly of me!

The spider holds a silver ball

The spider holds a silver ball
In unperceivèd hands
And dancing softly to himself
His yarn of pearl unwinds.

He plies from naught to naught
In unsubstantial trade,
Supplants our tapestries with his
In half the period —

An hour to rear supreme
His theories of light,
Then dangle from the housewife's broom,
His sophistries forgot.

unperceivèd — unseen
plies — works
naught — nothing
unsubstantial — unseen
tapestries — wall-hangings
sophistries — ideas

There's a certain slant of light

There's a certain slant of light,
On winter afternoons,
That oppresses, like the weight
Of cathedral tunes.

Heavenly hurt it gives us;
We can find no scar,
But internal difference
Where the meanings are.

None may teach it — Any —
'Tis the seal, despair, —
An imperial affliction
Sent us of the air.

When it comes, the landscape listens,
Shadows hold their breath;
When it goes 'tis like the distance
On the look of death.

oppresses — weighs down
imperial affliction — powerful pain or disturbance

31

The going from a world we know

The going from a world we know
To one a wonder still
Is like the child's adversity
Whose vista is a hill,
Behind the hill is sorcery
And everything unknown,
But will the secret compensate
For climbing it alone?

adversity — difficulty, struggle
vista — distant view
sorcery — witchcraft, magic
compensate — make up for

Like brooms of steel

Like brooms of steel
The Snow and Wind
Had swept the Winter Street,
The House was hooked,
The Sun sent out
Faint Deputies of heat–
Where rode the Bird
The Silence tied
His ample, plodding Steed,
The Apple in the cellar snug
Was all the one that played.

hooked — locked up
deputies — law-enforcers

I went to heaven

I went to heaven —
'Twas a small town —
Lit with a Ruby —
Lathed with down —
Stiller than the fields
At the full dew,
Beautiful as pictures
No man drew,
People like the moth
Of Mechlin frames —
Duties of gossamer
And eider names
Almost contented
I could be —
'Mong such unique
Society

lathed — covered
Mechlin frames — bodies made of fine lace
duties — clothing
eider — soft, like ducks' down
unique — one of a kind

34

Spring

New feet within my garden go

New feet within my garden go,
New fingers stir the sod;
A troubadour upon the elm
Betrays the solitude.

New children play upon the green,
New weary sleep below;
And still the pensive spring returns,
And still the punctual snow!

sod — earth
troubadour — old name given to a poet in France
betrays — upsets or reveals
pensive — thoughtful in a sad way
punctual — exact

Bee, I'm expecting you!

Bee, I'm expecting you!
Was saying yesterday
To somebody you know
That you were due.

The frogs got home last week,
Are settled and at work,
Birds mostly back,
The clover warm and thick.

You'll get my letter by
The seventeenth; reply,
Or better, be with me.
Yours,
Fly.

Hope is the thing with feathers

Hope is the thing with feathers
That perches in the soul,
And sings the tune without the words,
And never stops at all,

And sweetest in the gale is heard;
And sore must be the storm
That could abash the little bird
That kept so many warm.

I've heard it in the chillest land,
And on the strangest sea;
Yet, never, in extremity,
It asked a crumb of me.

abash — cause to be silent, or frighten
sore — hard or fierce
extremity — severe hardship

Nubria

Zanfara Regnum

2 Parigu

Belegau

Biafara

Tigremahon

Roum

Bagamidri

Baluum Ropuli

Anibes

Vanguc oru

Niger Fleuz

Medra

Will there really be a morning?

Will there really be a morning?
Is there such a thing as day?
Could I see it from the mountains
If I were as tall as they?

Has it feet like water-lilies?
Has it feathers like a bird?
Is it brought from famous countries
Of which I have never heard?

Oh some scholar! Oh some sailor!
Oh some wise man from the skies!
Please to tell a little pilgrim
Where the place called "morning" lies!

pilgrim — a wanderer or traveler, especially to a holy place

A word is dead

A word is dead
When it is said
Some say.
I say it just
Begins to live
That day.

40

I send two Sunsets

I send two Sunsets —
Day and I in competition ran.
I finished two, and several stars,
While he was making one.

His own was ampler —
But, as I was saying to a friend,
Mine is the more convenient
To carry in the hand.

The wind begun to rock the grass

The wind begun to rock the grass
With threatening tunes and low, —
He flung a menace at the earth,
A menace at the sky.

The leaves unhooked themselves from trees
And started all abroad;
The dust did scoop itself like hands
And throw away the road.

The wagons quickened on the streets,
The thunder hurried slow;
The lightning showed a yellow beak,
And then a livid claw.

The birds put up the bars to nests,
The cattle fled to barns;
There came one drop of giant rain,
And then, as if the hands

That held the dams had parted hold,
The waters wrecked the sky,
But overlooked my father's house,
Just quartering a tree.

menace — threat or curse
livid — fiery
quartering — breaking into four pieces

A curious cloud surprised the sky

A curious cloud surprised the sky,
'Twas like a sheet with horns;
The sheet was blue, the antlers gray,
It almost touched the lawns

So low it leaned, then statelier drew,
And trailed like robes away —
A queen adown a satin aisle
Had not the majesty.

44

adown — moving down

There is no frigate like a book

There is no frigate like a book
 To take us lands away,
Nor any coursers like a page
 Of prancing poetry.
This traverse may the poorest take
 Without oppress of toll;
How frugal is the chariot
 That bears a human soul!

frigate — boat
coursers — powerful horses
traverse — travel
oppress — burden
frugal — careful with money

What Emily Was Thinking

Summer

It's all I have to bring today: Emily offers a gift that includes her heart, the fields and meadows, then "all the bees." She says "this, and my heart" three times, as if speaking a magic charm.

In the name of the Bee: Emily crafts a blessing from three happy words beginning with "B"—the Bee, the Butterfly, and the Breeze, who live in her garden.

I'm nobody! Who are you?: The poet, "nobody," makes friends with another nobody. Unlike the "dreary" somebodies who brag about themselves, Emily has sneaky fun with the rhymes of "frog" and "bog."

A bird came down the walk: Secretly watching a bird gobble his angleworm lunch, Emily captures his nervous movements. As he refuses her "crumb" and leaps into the air, the bird seems to swim in light.

They dropped like Flakes: During the Civil War (1861–1865), which happened in Emily's lifetime, young men were killed. The poet grieved for them. Many disappeared and were never buried. But God, she says, knows who they are.

"Answer, July!": The seasons go by quickly! When Emily asks July where spring has gone, May reminds July of winter and early spring blue jays. When the fussy blue jay mentions the fall harvests, mists, and seed-pods, the Year speaks up to claim them all.

A narrow fellow in the grass: The poet sees a snake creeping through the grass. She knows its home and habits, and makes her poem slither down the page. The last line shivers in its cold rhymes of "zero" and "bone."

Exhilaration is the breeze: Speaking the word "exhilaration" lets us walk on air, until we come back to earth, refreshed by a magical joy.

To make a prairie it takes a clover and one bee: The poet liked to bake sweet treats. Here is her recipe for a meadow. The secret ingredient is daydream.

A soft sea washed around the house: The poet imagines her house sailing on an ocean of summer air, guided by a butterfly and a bee. As part of the universe, she gets to ride along.

From all the jails the boys and girls: School's out! Children are free to run and make noise. It's too bad that grownups don't like the "mob."

Autumn

The gentian weaves her fringes: In fall, the poet sees her garden prepare for the cold by weaving bright cloth. When the flowers depart, their vivid parade ends.

Faith is a fine invention: In this sharp and sassy poem, Emily challenges "gentlemen" who see religion as superior to science. A microscope lets her examine hidden worlds.

Blazing in gold and quenching in purple: The active words in the poem—which end in "ing"—create a circus out of a sunset, commanded by the "juggler of day," the sun.

I never saw a moor: Although she doesn't know the world far from home, the poet has an imagination. She can shut her eyes and be wherever she wishes to go.

He fumbles at your spirit: The poet captures the noisy music of a thunderstorm, as if trapped inside a huge piano. The sounds heighten the drama, until the thunderbolt delivers its mighty blow.

Because I could not stop for Death: A kind carriage driver takes the poet from life to death, past childhood scenes. At sunset, she sees that her final "house" lies in the burying ground, and that the driver has taken her toward "eternity," where time disappears into the journey.

The cricket sang: A cricket's song helps the sun finish its daily work. When night descends, the day, like a life, has ended in peace. The poem's gentle rhymes—"name," "home,"—create a hymn of farewell.

Winter

Safe in their alabaster chambers: Emily sees both underground, where the dead sleep, and into space, where stars and planets move like ships rowing on a vast sea. Even powerful rulers disappear, like "dots" of snow on a white field.

It sifts from leaden sieves: The snow whirls through this poem like an acrobat, or a theatrical designer, transforming the landscape, then twirling into nothing.

This is my letter to the world: At her small writing table facing the large bright windows, Emily beholds the trees, grass, and sky, and then returns to her letter to the world. Her words carry her love of Nature in its simple majesty. We must read "tenderly."

The spider holds a silver ball: Like a poet, a spider works unseen, "dancing softly," as he constructs his whole world. But one sweep of a broom makes it vanish.

There's a certain slant of light: A beam of winter sunlight stabs the poet with "heavenly hurt." Then the "shadows" deepen the distance between herself and her memories of those she has lost.

The going from a world we know: When we wonder where we go when we die, we imagine climbing up a hill by ourselves. Mysteries await us, but will knowing their secrets be worth the lonely struggle?

Like brooms of steel: The winter wind and snow scrape the street like steel brooms. Silence stands tied to a tree, like a big farm-horse. But, safely stored for the winter, the apple plays in the cellar. Perhaps Emily wanted to be the apple.

I went to heaven: This heaven is so quiet and soft that its charms and moth-like people seem almost unreal. Having visited this heaven in a dream or poem, she might be "almost" contented there.

Spring

New feet within my garden go: In spring, Emily sees how new creatures—birds, animals, neighbors—arrive in town. She often thinks of opposites: the young and the "weary," the spring green and the same ground covered with snow.

Bee, I'm expecting you!: Here's a letter-poem from a fly to a bee, giving the neighborhood news. Like someone writing to an absent friend, the poet commands the friend to "be with me," making a pun on "be"!

Hope is the thing with feathers: The poet sees hope as a brave bird that sings through storm, cold, and loneliness, yet never asks to be fed "a crumb." The giving comes from hope, and the poet speaks in grateful awe.

Will there really be a morning?: Six questions in twelve lines! The poem is like a game of hide-and-go-seek, with sly Emily in her little-girl costume, teasing the "wise" grown-ups.

A word is dead: In twenty syllables, the poet lets her words hatch into life. The only two-syllable word, "begins," wakes up human speech and gives it a good "day."

I send two Sunsets: The poem offers a gift, perhaps of poems about sunsets and stars, written in a contest with "Day." The day's sunset is larger, but hers are easier to carry.

The wind begun to rock the grass: A thunderstorm upsets everything—grass, sky, wagons, birds, and cattle. Every line of the poem jumps with energy, until the house is spared and only a tree lies broken apart.

A curious cloud surprised the sky: Seeing a strange cloud with horns or antlers, the poet watches it descend, then arise and move off. When it changes shape, it looks like a queen walking on a satin carpet.

There is no frigate like a book: Reading a poem can take us anywhere in the world, and the journey is free. Emily's poems take us to China, Peru, Brazil—even past the earth into the stars.

Bibliography

Definitions of words and phrases in some of the poems are adapted from The Emily Dickinson Lexicon, Cynthia Hallen, ed. http://edl.byu.edu/index.php, 2007.

Hampson, Alfred Leete, ed. *Emily Dickinson: Poems for Youth*. Foreword by Mary Lamberton Becker. Boston: Little, Brown and Co., 1934.

Poems of Emily Dickinson. Selected by Helen Plotz. New York: Thomas Y. Crowell Co., 1965.

Todd, Mabel Loomis, and Millicent Todd Bingham, eds. *Bolts of Melody: New Poems of Emily Dickinson*. New York: Harper and Brothers Publishers, 1945.

Unpublished Poems of Emily Dickinson, edited by her niece Martha Dickinson Bianchi and Alfred Leete Hampson. Boston: Little, Brown and Co., 1936.

Index

The Poetry Collection

Shakespeare

The Poetry Collection

Shakespeare

Edited by
Marguerite Tassi, PhD

Illustrated by
Mercè López

MoonDance

This book is dedicated to my wonderful children, Francesca and James. —M.T.

To Roberto and Frida —M.L.

Brimming with creative inspiration, how-to projects, and useful information to enrich your everyday life, Quarto Knows is a favorite destination for those pursuing their interests and passions. Visit our site and dig deeper with our books into your area of interest: Quarto Creates, Quarto Cooks, Quarto Homes, Quarto Lives, Quarto Drives, Quarto Explores, Quarto Gifts, or Quarto Kids.

© 2018 Quarto Publishing Group USA Inc.
Original text © 2018 Marguerite Tassi
Illustrations © 2018 Mercè López

First Published in 2017 by Published by MoonDance Press, an imprint of The Quarto Group.
26391 Crown Valley Parkway, Suite 220, Mission Viejo, CA 92691, USA.
T (949) 380-7510 **F** (949) 380-7575 **www.QuartoKnows.com**

Walter Foster Publishing titles are also available at discount for retail, wholesale, promotional, and bulk purchase. For details, contact the Special Sales Manager by email at specialsales@quarto.com or by mail at The Quarto Group, Attn: Special Sales Manager, 100 Cummings Center, Suite 265D, Beverly, MA 01915, USA.

ISBN: 978-1-63322-504-6

Digital edition published in 2018
eISBN: 978-1-63322-505-3

Cover design and layout by Melissa Gerber

Printed in Guangdong, China
10 9 8 7 6 5 4 3 2 1
November 2019
19090228

Contents

Introduction

WILLIAM SHAKESPEARE WAS AN ENGLISH PLAYWRIGHT, ACTOR, AND POET who lived during the reigns of two monarchs, Queen Elizabeth I and King James I. Widely regarded as the greatest writer in the English language, he has gained fame across the globe for his brilliance as a dramatist.

For all of his fame and fortune, William's beginnings were humble. He was born in April 1564 in Stratford, a small town on the River Avon one hundred miles from London. He was the oldest surviving child of John Shakespeare, a successful glove maker, and Mary Arden. William attended the King's New School in Stratford, taking classes six days a week, primarily in Latin grammar and literature, until about the age of fifteen. At age eighteen, William married a local girl, Anne Hathaway. They had three children: Susanna and twins named Judith and Hamnet. Sadly, Hamnet lived only to the age of eleven. By all appearances, William's life was relatively quiet until his mid-twenties when he left Stratford to try his fortune in the big city.

In the late 1580s, the London-area theatres were on the rise, teeming with excitement and life. William made his way to London to work in this vibrant artistic world, where a new show played every afternoon in gorgeously painted wooden playhouses. William got his start as an actor, but it did not take long for him to realize that his greatest talent lay in playwriting. He joined an acting company called the Lord Chamberlain's Men, later known as the King's Men (when James I became their patron). William became the company's resident dramatist at the Theatre, the first professionally built playhouse in London. The Lord Chamberlain's Men were a travelling company as well, which meant that William's plays were performed at inns, royal courts, universities, and in other English towns.

William first won fame with his history plays in the early 1590s, which brought the thrilling stories of England's kings to the stage. He then gained further popularity with comedies like *A Midsummer Night's Dream* and tragedies, such as *Romeo and Juliet* and *Hamlet*. His soaring poetry, lifelike characters, and dramatic innovations made William the most popular playwright of his time. He also earned a reputation as a poet, writing a number of long poems and 154 sonnets.

William is best known for his association with the Globe Theatre. When the Lord Chamberlain's Men lost their lease to the land under the Theatre, they took a risk that changed the course of history. In the dead of night, the men met at the Theatre, and despite the wintry cold, they worked to dismantle the entire building. Then they carried the timber across the frozen River Thames to another site, where the playhouse was rebuilt and named the Globe. Although it was demolished eventually in 1644, a new Globe playhouse was built many years later and opened in 1997.

William died a wealthy man in Stratford in April 1616 at the age of fifty-two. Seven years later, his friends from the King's Men, John Heminge and Henry Condell, did something that would change literary and theatrical history profoundly. They collected all of William's handwritten scripts and brought them to a printer. In 1623, the collected plays of Shakespeare, called the First Folio, appeared in print. Among the thirty-six plays were eighteen that would have been lost had they not appeared in the Folio, including some of William's best loved works: *Macbeth, Julius Caesar, As You Like It*, and *The Tempest*. As his friend and fellow 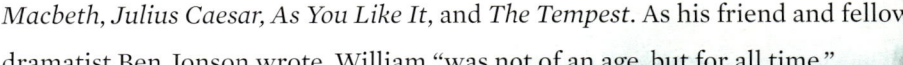 dramatist Ben Jonson wrote, William "was not of an age, but for all time."

All the World's a Stage

FROM *As You Like It,* ACT 2, SCENE 7

All the world's a stage,
And all the men and women merely players:
They have their exits and their entrances,
And one man in his time plays many parts,
His acts being seven ages. At first the infant,
Mewling and puking in the nurse's arms.
And then the whining school-boy, with his satchel
And shining morning face, creeping like snail
Unwillingly to school. And then the lover,
Sighing like furnace, with a woeful ballad
Made to his mistress' eyebrow. Then a soldier,
Full of strange oaths and bearded like the pard,
Jealous in honour, sudden and quick in quarrel,
Seeking the bubble reputation
Even in the cannon's mouth. And then the justice,
In fair round belly with good capon lined,
With eyes severe and beard of formal cut,
Full of wise saws and modern instances;
And so he plays his part.

The sixth age shifts
Into the lean and slipper'd pantaloon,
With spectacles on nose and pouch on side,
His youthful hose, well saved, a world too wide
For his shrunk shank; and his big manly voice,
Turning again toward childish treble, pipes
And whistles in his sound. Last scene of all,
That ends this strange eventful history,
Is second childishness and mere oblivion,
Sans teeth, sans eyes, sans taste, sans everything.

Mewling—whimpering
Like furnace—like a furnace emitting smoke
Bearded like the pard—having whiskers like a leopard
Jealous in honour—carefully guarding his honour
Bubble reputation—fleeting glory
Capon—cock fattened for eating; often presented to judges as a bribe
Saws—sayings
Modern instances—commonplace illustrations or proofs against universal beliefs
Pantaloon—ridiculous old merchant from Italian comedy
Hose—leggings
A world—far
Shank—leg
Mere oblivion—complete forgetfulness
Sans—without

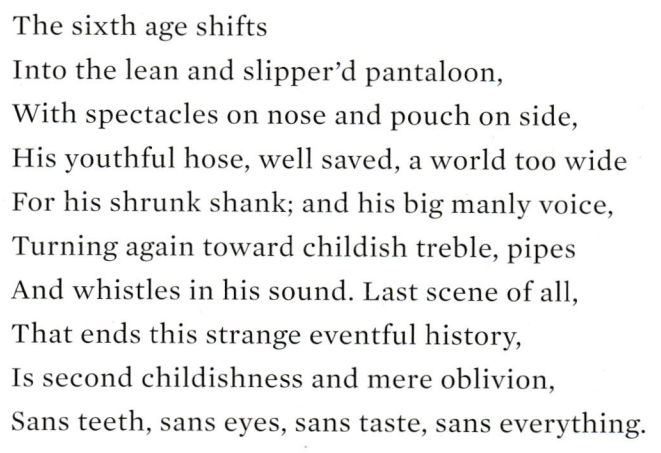

O, for a Muse of Fire

FROM *Henry V*, ACT 1, PROLOGUE

O, for a Muse of fire, that would ascend
The brightest heaven of invention,
A kingdom for a stage, princes to act
And monarchs to behold the swelling scene!
Then should the warlike Harry, like himself,
Assume the port of Mars; and at his heels,
Leash'd in like hounds, should famine, sword and fire
Crouch for employment. But pardon, and gentles all,
The flat unraised spirits that have dared
On this unworthy scaffold to bring forth
So great an object: can this cockpit hold
The vasty fields of France? or may we cram
Within this wooden O the very casques
That did affright the air at Agincourt?
O, pardon! since a crooked figure may
Attest in little place a million;
And let us, ciphers to this great accompt,

On your imaginary forces work.
Suppose within the girdle of these walls
Are now confined two mighty monarchies,
Whose high upreared and abutting fronts
The perilous Narrow Ocean parts asunder:
Piece out our imperfections with your thoughts;
Into a thousand parts divide one man,
And make imaginary puissance;
Think when we talk of horses, that you see them
Printing their proud hoofs i' th' receiving earth;
For 'tis your thoughts that now must deck our kings,
Carry them here and there; jumping o'er times,
Turning the accomplishment of many years
Into an hour-glass: for the which supply,
Admit me Chorus to this history;
Who Prologue-like your humble patience pray,
Gently to hear, kindly to judge, our play.

Muse—source of inspiration
Invention—imagination
Swelling—increasing in magnificence
Port—appearance
Scaffold—stage's platform
Wooden O—a circular amphitheatre
Very casque—actual helmets
Agincourt—a village in Northern France
   where Henry V won his greatest victory
Crooked figure—zero
Attest—stand for
Narrow Ocean—the English Channel
Ciphers—zeroes
Parts—actors' roles
Puissance—armies

We Were, Fair Queen

FROM *The Winter's Tale*, ACT 1, SCENE 2

Behind—to come
Changed—exchanged
Ill-doing—sin
Reared—raised
Weak spirits—youthful vital powers
Stronger blood—adult emotions, passions
The imposition cleared/Hereditary ours—the burden of original sin is not ours. In Christianity, it was thought that humans were born with sin because Adam and Eve disobeyed God.

We were, fair Queen,
Two lads that thought there was no more behind
But such a day to-morrow as to-day,
And to be boy eternal.
We were as twinn'd lambs that did frisk i' th' sun,
And bleat the one at th' other. What we changed
Was innocence for innocence. We knew not
The doctrine of ill-doing, nor dream'd
That any did. Had we pursued that life,
And our weak spirits ne'er been higher rear'd
With stronger blood, we should have answer'd heaven
Boldly, 'Not guilty', the imposition clear'd
Hereditary ours.

Over Hill, Over Dale

FROM *A Midsummer Night's Dream*, ACT 2, SCENE 1

Over hill, over dale,
    Thorough bush, thorough briar,
Over park, over pale,
    Thorough flood, thorough fire,
I do wander everywhere,
Swifter than the moon's sphere;
And I serve the Fairy Queen,
To dew her orbs upon the green.
The cowslips tall her pensioners be:
In their gold coats spots you see;
Those be rubies, fairy favours,
In those freckles live their savours:
I must go seek some dewdrops here
And hang a pearl in every cowslip's ear.

Dale—a wide, open valley
Thorough—through
Pale—fenced-in area
Moon's sphere—In Ptolemaic
  astronomy, it was thought
  that the moon was carried
  around the earth in its own
  transparent crystal globe.
Orbs—circles of dark grass
  where fairies danced
Cowslips—yellow flowers
Pensioners—the royal
  bodyguards, dressed in bright
  colours
Savours—fragrance

Round About the Cauldron Go

FROM *Macbeth*, ACT 4, SCENE 1

Round about the cauldron go;
In the poison'd entrails throw.
Toad, that under cold stone
Days and nights has thirty-one
Swelter'd venom sleeping got,
Boil thou first i' th' charmed pot.

Double, double, toil and trouble;
Fire burn, and cauldron bubble.

Fillet of a fenny snake,
In the cauldron boil and bake.
Eye of newt, and toe of frog,
Wool of bat, and tongue of dog,
Adder's fork, and blind-worm's sting,
Lizard's leg, and owlet's wing,
For a charm of powerful trouble,
Like a hell-broth, boil and bubble.

Double, double, toil and trouble;
Fire burn, and cauldron bubble.

Swelter'd venom sleeping got—releases poison
*   formed during sleep*
Toil—hard work, dispute
Fillet—slice
Fenny—from the marshlands
Fork—poisonous split tongue
Blind-worm—an adder

Under the Greenwood Tree

FROM *As You Like It,* ACT 2, SCENE 5

Under the greenwood tree,
    Who loves to lie with me,
And turn his merry note
    Unto the sweet bird's throat;
Come hither, come hither, come hither:
    Here shall he see
    No enemy
But winter and rough weather.

Who doth ambition shun
    And loves to live i' th' sun,
Seeking the food he eats,
    And pleased with what he gets;
Come hither, come hither, come hither:
    Here shall he see
    No enemy
But winter and rough weather.

Turn—tune, adapt
Throat—voice
Live i' th' sun—free from care

Shall I Compare Thee to a Summer's Day?

SONNET 18

Shall I compare thee to a summer's day?

Thou art more lovely and more temperate:

Rough winds do shake the darling buds of May,

And summer's lease hath all too short a date:

Sometime too hot the eye of heaven shines,

And often is his gold complexion dimm'd;

And every fair from fair sometime declines,

By chance or nature's changing course untrimm'd;

But thy eternal summer shall not fade

Nor lose possession of that fair thou ow'st;

Nor shall Death brag thou wander'st in his shade,

When in eternal lines to time thou grow'st:

    So long as men can breathe or eyes can see,

    So long lives this, and this gives life to thee.

Temperate—mild
Lease—time allowed
Date—duration
The eye of heaven—the sun
Every fair from fair sometime declines—everything beautiful loses its beauty
Untrimm'd—stripped of its beauty
Ow'st—own
Lines—lines of poetry
Thou grow'st—you become part of the poem and, therefore, of time
This—the poem

O Romeo, Romeo, Wherefore Art Thou Romeo?

FROM *Romeo and Juliet,* ACT 2, SCENE 2

O Romeo, Romeo, wherefore art thou Romeo?
Deny thy father and refuse thy name;
Or, if thou wilt not, be but sworn my love,
And I'll no longer be a Capulet.
'Tis but thy name that is my enemy;
Thou art thyself, though not a Montague.
What's Montague? It is nor hand, nor foot,
Nor arm, nor face, nor any other part
Belonging to a man. O, be some other name!
What's in a name? That which we call a rose
By any other name would smell as sweet;
So Romeo would, were he not Romeo call'd,
Retain that dear perfection which he owes
Without that title. Romeo, doff thy name,
And for thy name which is no part of thee
Take all myself.

Wherefore—why
Though—even if
Owes—owns
Doff—cast aside

Now Is the Winter of Our Discontent

FROM *Richard III,* ACT 1, SCENE 1

Now is the winter of our discontent
Made glorious summer by this son of York;
And all the clouds that low'r'd upon our house
In the deep bosom of the ocean buried.
Now are our brows bound with victorious wreaths;
Our bruised arms hung up for monuments;
Our stern alarums changed to merry meetings,
Our dreadful marches to delightful measures.
Grim-visaged War hath smooth'd his wrinkled front;
And now, instead of mounting barbed steeds
To fright the souls of fearful adversaries,
He capers nimbly in a lady's chamber
To the lascivious pleasing of a lute.
But I, that am not shaped for sportive tricks,
Nor made to court an amorous looking-glass;
I, that am rudely stamp'd, and want love's majesty
To strut before a wanton ambling nymph;
I, that am curtail'd of this fair proportion,

Cheated of feature by dissembling nature,
Deformed, unfinish'd, sent before my time
Into this breathing world, scarce half made up,
And that so lamely and unfashionable
That dogs bark at me as I halt by them;
Why, I, in this weak piping time of peace,
Have no delight to pass away the time,
Unless to see my shadow in the sun
And descant on mine own deformity:
And therefore, since I cannot prove a lover,
To entertain these fair well-spoken days,
I am determined to prove a villain
And hate the idle pleasures of these days.

Son of York—in British history, Edward IV, son of Richard, Duke of York
Low'r'd—frowned
Bruised arms—battered weapons, armour
Alarums—summons to battle by drums and trumpets
Measures—melodies, stately dances
Wrinkled front—frowning forehead
Capers nimbly—leaps quickly and lightly in dance
Lascivious—desirable
Sportive tricks—playful games
Rudely stamped—roughly shaped
Want—lack
Wanton ambling—playfully strolling
Nymph—beautiful young woman
Curtailed—deprived
Feature—bodily shape
Dissembling—deceitful
Sent before my time—born prematurely
Piping—sounding like a pipe, or wind instrument
Descant—sing or play variations on a musical theme, comment on

If Music Be the Food of Love

FROM *Twelfth Night,* ACT 1, SCENE 1

If music be the food of love, play on;
Give me excess of it, that, surfeiting,
The appetite may sicken, and so die.
That strain again! it had a dying fall.
O, it came o'er my ear like the sweet sound
That breathes upon a bank of violets,
Stealing and giving odour! Enough; no more:
'Tis not so sweet now as it was before.
O spirit of love! how quick and fresh art thou,
That, notwithstanding thy capacity
Receiveth as the sea, nought enters there,
Of what validity and pitch so e'er,
But falls into abatement and low price,
Even in a minute! So full of shapes is fancy
That it alone is high fantastical.

Surfeiting—consuming too much
That strain again—(to the musicians)
  play that musical phrase again
Dying fall—fading away
Quick and fresh—alive and eager, hungry
Capacity/Receiveth as the sea—able to
  take in impressions as vast as the sea
Validity and pitch—high value
Abatement—decline
Shapes—imagined forms
Fancy—love
High fantastical—highly imaginative,
  very passionate

How Sweet the Moonlight Sleeps Upon This Bank!

FROM *The Merchant of Venice*, ACT 5, SCENE 1

How sweet the moonlight sleeps upon this bank!
Here will we sit and let the sounds of music
Creep in our ears: soft stillness and the night
Become the touches of sweet harmony.
Sit, Jessica. Look how the floor of heaven
Is thick inlaid with patens of bright gold:
There's not the smallest orb which thou behold'st
But in his motion like an angel sings,
Still quiring to the young-eyed cherubins;
Such harmony is in immortal souls;
But whilst this muddy vesture of decay
Doth grossly close it in, we cannot hear it.

Bank—a slope of land alongside a river
Become—suit
Touches—musical notes
Floor of heaven—the sky
Patens—shallow dishes
Motion of the orbs—the belief that the concentric circles of the Ptolemaic spheres created harmonious music by their movement (known as the music of the spheres), which cannot be heard by mortals
Still quiring—continually singing together
Cherubins—angels
Muddy vesture of decay—the body
Doth grossly close it in—does physically enclose an immortal soul

O, She Doth Teach the Torches to Burn Bright!

FROM *Romeo and Juliet*, ACT 1, SCENE 5

O, she doth teach the torches to burn bright!
It seems she hangs upon the cheek of night
Like a rich jewel in an Ethiope's ear;
Beauty too rich for use, for earth too dear!
So shows a snowy dove trooping with crows,
As yonder lady o'er her fellows shows.
The measure done, I'll watch her place of stand,
And, touching hers, make blessed my rude hand.
Did my heart love till now? forswear it, sight!
For I ne'er saw true beauty till this night.

Doth—does
Ethiope—Ethiopian, black African
Beauty too rich for use, for earth too dear—beauty that is too precious for this
    world
Trooping—flocking
Measure—dance
Forswear—break a former oath

O Mistress Mine, Where Are You Roaming?

FROM *Twelfth Night*, ACT 2, SCENE 3

O mistress mine, where are you roaming?
O, stay and hear; your true love's coming,
That can sing both high and low.
Trip no further, pretty sweeting;
Journeys end in lovers meeting,
Every wise man's son doth know.

What is love? 'Tis not hereafter;
Present mirth hath present laughter;
What's to come is still unsure.
In delay there lies no plenty;
Then come kiss me, sweet and twenty;
Youth's a stuff will not endure.

Mistress—girlfriend, beloved
Still—always
Sweet and twenty—sweet and twenty times sweet

24

What Light Is Light, if Silvia Be Not Seen?

FROM *The Two Gentlemen of Verona*, ACT 3, SCENE 1

What light is light, if Silvia be not seen?
What joy is joy, if Silvia be not by?
Unless it be to think that she is by
And feed upon the shadow of perfection
Except I be by Silvia in the night,
There is no music in the nightingale;
Unless I look on Silvia in the day,
There is no day for me to look upon.

Shadow—image

But Soft, What Light Through Yonder Window Breaks?

FROM *Romeo and Julet,* ACT 2, SCENE 2

But soft, what light through yonder window breaks?

It is the east, and Juliet is the sun.

Arise, fair sun, and kill the envious moon,

Who is already sick and pale with grief,

That thou her maid art far more fair than she:

Be not her maid, since she is envious;

Her vestal livery is but sick and green

And none but fools do wear it; cast it off.

It is my lady, O, it is my love!

O, that she knew she were!

She speaks yet she says nothing: what of that?

Her eye discourses; I will answer it.

I am too bold, 'tis not to me she speaks:

Two of the fairest stars in all the heaven,

Having some business, do entreat her eyes

To twinkle in their spheres till they return.

What if her eyes were there, they in her head?

The brightness of her cheek would shame those stars,

As daylight doth a lamp; her eyes in heaven

Would through the airy region stream so bright

That birds would sing and think it were not night.

See, how she leans her cheek upon her hand!

O, that I were a glove upon that hand,

That I might touch that cheek!

Soft—wait
Her maid—a follower of Diana,
*   goddess of the moon*
Vestal livery—pure clothing,
*   appearance*
Sick and green—anemia suffered by
*   young girls, paleness*
Discourses—speaks
Stars—planets
There—in the stars' spheres
Airy region—heavens

26

My Mistress' Eyes Are Nothing Like the Sun

SONNET 130

My mistress' eyes are nothing like the sun;

Coral is far more red than her lips' red;

If snow be white, why then her breasts are dun;

If hairs be wires, black wires grow on her head.

I have seen roses damask'd, red and white,

But no such roses see I in her cheeks;

And in some perfumes is there more delight

Than in the breath that from my mistress reeks.

I love to hear her speak, yet well I know

That music hath a far more pleasing sound;

I grant I never saw a goddess go;

My mistress, when she walks, treads on the ground.

    And yet, by heaven, I think my love as rare

    As any she belied with false compare.

Dun—dull grey-brown
Damask'd—ornamented with streaks of color
Reeks—exhales (not necessarily an unpleasant smell)
Go—walk
Rare—special
Any she belied with false compare—any woman lied about in poetry

The Lunatic, the Lover, and the Poet

FROM *A Midsummer Night's Dream*, ACT 5, SCENE 1

The lunatic, the lover, and the poet

Are of imagination all compact.

One sees more devils than vast hell can hold:

That is the madman. The lover, all as frantic,

Sees Helen's beauty in a brow of Egypt.

The poet's eye, in a fine frenzy rolling,

Doth glance from heaven to earth, from earth to heaven,

And, as imagination bodies forth

The forms of things unknown, the poet's pen

Turns them to shapes, and gives to airy nothing

A local habitation and a name.

Such tricks hath strong imagination,

That if it would but apprehend some joy,

It comprehends some bringer of that joy;

Or in the night, imagining some fear,

How easy is a bush supposed a bear!

Compact—composed

Helen's beauty—alluding to the legendary beauty of the blonde and fair-skinned Helen of Troy

A brow of Egypt—the dark-complexioned face of a woman from Egypt

Airy nothing—the insubstantial stuff of the imagination

Local habitation—through writing, the poet creates a place for the imagination to take form.

Apprehend—imagine

Bringer—the source

29

Let Me Not to the Marriage of True Minds

SONNET 116

Let me not to the marriage of true minds
Admit impediments. Love is not love
Which alters when it alteration finds,
Or bends with the remover to remove.
O no! it is an ever-fixed mark
That looks on tempests and is never shaken;
It is the star to every wand'ring bark,
Whose worth's unknown, although his height be taken.
Love's not Time's fool, though rosy lips and cheeks
Within his bending sickle's compass come:
Love alters not with his brief hours and weeks,
But bears it out even to the edge of doom.
    If this be error and upon me proved,
    I never writ, nor no man ever loved.

Let me not—may I never

Admit impediments—allow objections (referring to the marriage service)

Bends with the remover to remove—inclining to change affections when the beloved does

Ever-fixed mark—a signal or beacon for ships to aid in navigation

Star—the guiding North Star

Wand'ring bark—lost ship

Whose worth's unknown—the value of which is beyond human measurement

His height be taken—altitude scientifically measured

Time's fool—something mocked by Time because Time has power over it

His bending sickle—the image of Time, like Death the Reaper, with a curved-edged farming tool

Upon me proved—proved against me

Cowards Die Many Times Before Their Deaths

FROM *Julius Caesar*, ACT 2, SCENE 2

Cowards die many times before their deaths;
The valiant never taste of death but once.
Of all the wonders that I yet have heard,
It seems to me most strange that men should fear,
Seeing that death, a necessary end,
Will come when it will come.

Once More Unto the Breach

FROM *Henry V*, ACT 3, SCENE 1

Once more unto the breach, dear friends, once more;
Or close the wall up with our English dead.
In peace there's nothing so becomes a man
As modest stillness and humility,
But when the blast of war blows in our ears,
Then imitate the action of the tiger.
Stiffen the sinews, conjure up the blood,
Disguise fair nature with hard-favour'd rage.
Then lend the eye a terrible aspect;
Let it pry through the portage of the head
Like the brass cannon; let the brow o'erwhelm it
As fearfully as doth a galled rock
O'erhang and jutty his confounded base,
Swill'd with the wild and wasteful ocean.
Now set the teeth and stretch the nostril wide,
Hold hard the breath, and bend up every spirit
To his full height. . .
I see you stand like greyhounds in the slips,
Straining upon the start. The game's afoot.
Follow your spirit, and upon this charge
Cry 'God for Harry, England and Saint George!'

Breach—a gap in a wall made by an attacking army
Fair nature—naturally handsome appearance
Hard-favour'd—stern-faced
Aspect—look
Let it pry through the portage—let the eye look
   through its socket
O'erwhelm—overhang the eyes with frowning
Galled—worn
Jutty—project over

Confounded—worn away
Swill'd—vigorously washed
Greyhounds on the slips—hunting dogs on leashes
The game's afoot—the prey are running
Harry, England and Saint George—the standard
   battle cry for England's army; Saint George is
   England's patron saint.

All Furnish'd, All in Arms

FROM *Henry IV, Part 1*, ACT 4, SCENE 1

All furnish'd, all in arms;
All plumed like ostriches, that with the wind
Baited like eagles having lately bathed;
Glittering in golden coats like images;
As full of spirit as the month of May,
And gorgeous as the sun at midsummer;
Wanton as youthful goats, wild as young bulls.
I saw young Harry with his beaver on,
His cuisses on his thighs, gallantly arm'd
Rise from the ground like feather'd Mercury,
And vaulted with such ease into his seat,
As if an angel dropp'd down from the clouds,
To turn and wind a fiery Pegasus,
And witch the world with noble horsemanship.

Furnish'd—dressed
Plumed—referring to feathers in a helmet
Baited—beating their wings
Golden coats—richly embroidered garments worn
  over armour
Images—pictures or statues illuminated with gold
Wanton—frisky
Beaver—helmet
Cuisses—thigh armour
Feather'd Mercury—the messenger of the gods in
  Roman mythology, represented with wings on
  his heels and cap
Wind—wheel about
Pegasus—winged horse of Greek mythology
Witch—bewitch

34

Strain'd—forced
Becomes—dignifies, graces
Sceptre—the monarch's staff,
  symbol of power
Temporal—earthly
Attribute to—outward show of
Seasons—softens

The Quality of Mercy Is Not Strain'd

FROM *The Merchant of Venice*, ACT 4, SCENE 1

The quality of mercy is not strain'd.
It droppeth as the gentle rain from heaven
Upon the place beneath. It is twice blest:
It blesseth him that gives, and him that takes.
'Tis mightiest in the mightiest; it becomes
The throned monarch better than his crown.
His sceptre shows the force of temporal power,
The attribute to awe and majesty,
Wherein doth sit the dread and fear of kings;
But mercy is above this sceptred sway.
It is enthroned in the hearts of kings;
It is an attribute to God himself;
And earthly power doth then show likest God's
When mercy seasons justice.

Friends, Romans, Countrymen, Lend Me Your Ears

FROM *Julius Caesar*, ACT 3, SCENE 2

Friends, Romans, countrymen, lend me your ears.
I come to bury Caesar, not to praise him.
The evil that men do lives after them;
The good is oft interred with their bones.
So let it be with Caesar. The noble Brutus
Hath told you Caesar was ambitious.
If it were so, it was a grievous fault,
And grievously hath Caesar answer'd it.
Here, under leave of Brutus and the rest
(For Brutus is an honourable man,
So are they all, all honourable men),
Come I to speak in Caesar's funeral.
He was my friend, faithful and just to me.
But Brutus says he was ambitious,
And Brutus is an honourable man.

He hath brought many captives home to Rome,

Whose ransoms did the general coffers fill.

Did this in Caesar seem ambitious?

When that the poor have cried, Caesar hath wept.

Ambition should be made of sterner stuff.

Yet Brutus says he was ambitious,

And Brutus is an honourable man.

You all did see that on the Lupercal

I thrice presented him a kingly crown,

Which he did thrice refuse: was this ambition?

Yet Brutus says he was ambitious,

And sure he is an honourable man.

I speak not to disprove what Brutus spoke,

But here I am to speak what I do know.

You all did love him once, not without cause.

What cause withholds you then to mourn for him?

O judgement! thou art fled to brutish beasts,

And men have lost their reason. Bear with me.

My heart is in the coffin there with Caesar,

And I must pause till it come back to me.

Interred—buried
General coffers—public treasury
Lupercal—refers to an ancient religious festival held in Rome to purify the city
Brutish—wordplay on Brutus's name

All That Glitters Is Not Gold

FROM *The Merchant of Venice*, ACT 2, SCENE 7

All that glitters is not gold;
Often have you heard that told.
Many a man his life hath sold
But my outside to behold.
Gilded tombs do worms enfold.

But my outside—only the exterior gold
Gilded—glittering with gold
Tombs do worms infold—tombs enclose worms

That Time of Year Thou Mayst in Me Behold

SONNET 73

That time of year thou mayst in me behold,
When yellow leaves, or none, or few, do hang
Upon those boughs which shake against the cold,
Bare ruin'd choirs where late the sweet birds sang.
In me thou seest the twilight of such day
As after sunset fadeth in the west,
Which by and by black night doth take away,
Death's second self that seals up all in rest.
In me thou seest the glowing of such fire
That on the ashes of his youth doth lie,
As the death-bed whereon it must expire,
Consumed with that which it was nourish'd by.
   This thou perceiv'st, which makes thy love more strong,
   To love that well, which thou must leave ere long.

*Bare ruin'd choirs—the tree's branches imagined as
   bare, without the singing birds of spring and summer*
Death's second self—sleep

39

To Be, or Not to Be, That Is the Question

FROM *Hamlet,* ACT 3, SCENE 1

To be, or not to be, that is the question:
Whether 'tis nobler in the mind to suffer
The slings and arrows of outrageous fortune,
Or to take arms against a sea of troubles,
And by opposing end them. To die, to sleep—
No more; and by a sleep to say we end
The heart-ache and the thousand natural shocks
That flesh is heir to; 'tis a consummation
Devoutly to be wish'd. To die, to sleep—
To sleep, perchance to dream. Ay, there's the rub;
For in that sleep of death what dreams may come
When we have shuffled off this mortal coil,
Must give us pause. There's the respect
That makes calamity of so long life.
For who would bear the whips and scorns of time,
Th' oppressor's wrong, the proud man's contumely,
The pangs of despised love, the law's delay,
The insolence of office, and the spurns
That patient merit of th' unworthy takes,
When he himself might his quietus make
With a bare bodkin? Who would fardels bear,
To grunt and sweat under a weary life,
But that the dread of something after death,
The undiscover'd country from whose bourn
No traveller returns, puzzles the will,
And makes us rather bear those ills we have

Than fly to others that we know not of?
Thus conscience does make cowards of us all;
And thus the native hue of resolution
Is sicklied o'er with the pale cast of thought,
And enterprises of great pitch and moment
With this regard their currents turn awry,
And lose the name of action. Soft you now,
The fair Ophelia? Nymph, in thy orisons
Be all my sins remember'd.

Outrageous—violent, cruel
Consummation—an ending
Rub—obstacle
Shuffled off this mortal coil—to die
Respect—consideration
Contumely—contempt
Office—people who hold an office
Spurns—scornful rejections
Quietus—release
Bare bodkin—a mere dagger
Fardels—burdens
Bourn—boundary
Native hue—natural colour
Cast—shade, tint
Pitch—aspiration, scope
Moment—importance
Turn awry—turning away from its course
Soft you—wait a moment
Orisons—prayers

Blow, Winds, and Crack Your Cheeks!

FROM *King Lear,* ACT 3, SCENE 2

Blow, winds, and crack your cheeks! Rage, blow,
You cataracts and hurricanoes, spout
Till you have drench'd our steeples, drown'd the cocks!
You sulph'rous and thought-executing fires,
Vaunt-couriers to oak-cleaving thunderbolts,
Singe my white head! And thou, all-shaking thunder,
Smite flat the thick rotundity o' the world!
Crack nature's moulds, all germens spill at once,
That make ingrateful man!

Crack your cheeks—winds personified as faces with puffed-out cheeks
Cataracts—floodgates of the heavens
Hurricanoes—water spouts
Drench'd—submerged
Cocks—weathervanes at the top of church steeples
Thought-executing fires—lightning (quick as thought)
Vaunt-couriers—forerunners
Smite flat—hit with great force (flatten)
Crack nature's moulds—destroy the molds that nature uses to create humans
Germens—seeds
Spill—destroy
Ingrateful—ungrateful

To-morrow, and To-morrow, and To-morrow

FROM *Macbeth*, ACT 5, SCENE 5

To-morrow, and to-morrow, and to-morrow
Creeps in this petty pace from day to day
To the last syllable of recorded time;
And all our yesterdays have lighted fools
The way to dusty death. Out, out, brief candle!
Life's but a walking shadow, a poor player
That struts and frets his hour upon the stage
And then is heard no more. It is a tale
Told by an idiot, full of sound and fury,
Signifying nothing.

Petty—meaningless
Syllable—merest trace
Poor player—bad actor
Frets—consumes

43

Why, Man, He Doth Bestride the Narrow World

FROM *Julius Caesar*, ACT 1, SCENE 2

Why, man, he doth bestride the narrow world
Like a Colossus, and we petty men
Walk under his huge legs and peep about
To find ourselves dishonourable graves.
Men at some time are masters of their fates.
The fault, dear Brutus, is not in our stars,
But in ourselves, that we are underlings.

Bestride—straddle
Colossus—legendary giant statue
Stars—astrological influences that were
    thought to determine fate

If We Shadows Have Offended

FROM *A Midsummer Night's Dream*, ACT 5, SCENE 1

If we shadows have offended,
Think but this, and all is mended,
That you have but slumber'd here
While these visions did appear.
And this weak and idle theme,
No more yielding but a dream,
Gentles, do not reprehend.
If you pardon, we will mend,
And, as I am an honest Puck,
If we have unearned luck
Now to 'scape the serpent's tongue,
We will make amends ere long;
Else the Puck a liar call.
So, good night unto you all.
Give me your hands, if we be friends,
And Robin shall restore amends.

Shadows—actors
No more yielding but a dream—with no more substance
  than a dream
Gentles—the audience
Reprehend—express disapproval
Mend—improve
'Scape the serpent's tongue—escape hissing
  from the audience
Give me your hands—applaud

45

Our Revels Now Are Ended

FROM *The Tempest*, ACT 4, SCENE 1

Our revels now are ended. These our actors,
As I foretold you, were all spirits and
Are melted into air, into thin air;
And, like the baseless fabric of this vision,
The cloud-capp'd towers, the gorgeous palaces,
The solemn temples, the great globe itself,
Yea, all which it inherit, shall dissolve,
And, like this insubstantial pageant faded,
Leave not a rack behind. We are such stuff
As dreams are made on, and our little life
Is rounded with a sleep.

Revels—the dance at the end of courtly entertainments
Baseless fabric—without substance
Globe—the world (alluding to the Globe Theatre)
Which it inherit—all those who occupy the earth
Pageant—scene, performance
Rack—cloud
Made on—made of
Rounded—surrounded

What William Was Thinking

All the World's a Stage: Theatre is the inspiration for this vision of the seven ages of man. In humorous detail, a parade of players appears, from the puking infant to the senile old man.

O, for a Muse of Fire: In the prologue to a history play featuring King Harry's conquest of France, an actor calls for inspiration. He asks the audience to use their imaginations to help fill in what the theater cannot show, such as vast fields of war.

We Were, Fair Queen: Two kings are remembering their childhood days when they were innocent and thought they would be boys forever.

Over Hill, Over Dale: Robin Goodfellow—a woodland elf from English folklore—travels the countryside serving the Fairy Queen, spreading dew on the grass and in the flowers.

Round About the Cauldron Go: Three witches brew up a powerful spell over their cauldron.

Under the Greenwood Tree: This lovely song invites us to celebrate a carefree life in nature.

Shall I Compare Thee to a Summer's Day: A poet wants to compare the beauty of his beloved to a summer's day. However, he realizes that summer can be unpleasant and that the seasons change. He envisions his love's beauty as an "eternal summer," which continually renews itself every time someone reads this poem.

O Romeo, Romeo, Wherefore Art Thou Romeo?: Juliet questions why she and Romeo must be bound to their names. Because their families are feuding (Capulets versus Montague), their names identify them as enemies. Juliet wishes that Romeo could discard his name so they could be together.

Now Is the Winter of Our Discontent: Richard, Duke of Gloucester, celebrates the victory of his family, the Yorks, in the Wars of the Roses. But when he thinks of his physical deformity, he feels bitter and decides to play the villain. Through violence, he will rise in power to become the infamous Richard III.

If Music Be the Food of Love: A lovesick man laments how music cannot cure him of his romantic passion. However, he compares the spirit of love to the sea.

How Sweet the Moonlight Sleeps Upon this Bank!: A young man and his love look at the beauty of the moonlit sky. He imagines that they can hear heavenly music in the night.

O, She Doth Teach the Torches to Burn Bright!: When Romeo catches his first glimpse of Juliet, he falls in love. Overwhelmed by her beauty, he imagines her as a bright light, a rich jewel, and a snowy dove.

O Mistress Mine, Where Are You Roaming?: This song celebrates the journey of love, which is best experienced when one is young.

What Light Is Light, If Silvia Be Not Seen?: A young man expresses such intense love that everything pales in the absence of his beloved. The best he can do is satisfy himself with the thought of her, which is just a "shadow" of the woman herself.

But Soft, What Light Through Yonder Window Breaks?: Romeo sees Juliet on her balcony. He imagines her as a brilliant source of light in the dark. She is the rising sun, more beautiful and vibrant than the pale moon, and her eyes are stars that might light up the sky.

My Mistress' Eyes Are Nothing Like the Sun: A poet creates a playful sonnet that mocks traditional love poems. Instead of praising his lady, he "dispraises" all of her parts. In the end, he declares his beloved just as "rare" as any of the ladies praised in poetry, which is the closest he comes to a declaration of love.

The Lunatic, the Lover, and the Poet: Imagination is a quality shared by madmen, lovers, and poets, who all see things that are not visible to the rational mind. The poet's genius lies in creating something out of nothing and giving it a name and a place to live in poetry and drama.

Let Me Not to the Marriage of True Minds: In this sonnet, the poet makes a declaration of true love, which remains constant in a world of change. In the final lines, the poet offers himself—and his poem—as proof that true love exists.

Cowards Die Many Times Before Their Deaths: Julius Caesar condemns cowards and praises the valiant who recognize that death is not to be feared.

Once More Unto the Breach: In his war against France, King Harry rouses his men to battle. He calls upon them to imitate the ferocity of a tiger.

All Furnish'd, All in Arms: This speech praises Harry (then a prince, soon to be king) by admiring his splendid armor and noble horsemanship.

The Quality of Mercy Is Not Strain'd: In William's play *The Merchant of Venice*, a young woman disguises herself as a lawyer to argue a case against a vengeful moneylender. Mercy, she declares, is a divine quality that blesses the giver and the receiver. Kings have earthly power, but they are most like God when they show mercy.

Friends, Romans, Countrymen, Lend Me Your Ears: In his funeral oration for Julius Caesar, Mark Antony refutes Brutus's accusation that Caesar was ambitious for the throne, and therefore deserved to be assassinated.

All That Glitters Is Not Gold: This wise saying reflects on how easily men are fooled by gold and exterior shows of wealth. Men have lost their lives in pursuit of all that dazzles the eye.

That Time of Year Thou Mayst in Me Behold: An aging poet using images of decay—the bare tree in winter, a fading sunset, and a dying fire—to acknowledge how strong his friend's love must be as the poet approaches his death.

To Be, or Not to Be, That Is the Question: Hamlet's contemplation of life and death is the most famous speech in theatre history. He fears what is to come in the afterlife and therefore hesitates to take his own life.

Blow, Winds, and Crack Your Cheeks!: Standing in the middle of a violent storm, King Lear calls upon the rain, thunder, and lightning to rage just as he is raging at the ingratitude of his daughters.

To-morrow, and To-morrow, and To-morrow: At his bleakest moment, Macbeth sees his life as a procession of meaningless days. He imagines himself as an actor playing his part for an hour on the stage, and then exiting to be heard no more.

Why, Man, He Doth Bestride the Narrow World: This vision of Julius Caesar as a gigantic statue whose legs straddle the world renders all of his followers as little, insignificant men. Cassius counsels Brutus to master his own destiny, rather than believe in the "stars" (fate).

If We Shadows Have Offended: Robin Goodfellow, a mischievous elf also known as Puck, speaks these final lines to the audience of *A Midsummer Night's Dream*, apologizing for anything in the play the actors ("shadows") have done that seemed offensive. He asks them to regard the play as nothing more than a dream.

Our Revels Now Are Ended: In William's last play, *The Tempest*, he reflects on how theatre is like life. Prospero, a mighty magician, has conjured spirits to perform a scene, and now that he has dismissed them, they disappear without a trace. So too, our brief life vanishes like a dream.

Index